JAPANESE COUNTRY QUILTING

JAPANESE COUNTRY QUILTING

Sashiko Patterns and Projects for Beginners

KAREN KIM MATSUNAGA

KODANSHA INTERNATIONAL LTD.
Tokyo & New York

To my grandmothers,
Masuyo Nakai and Miriam Watanabe

The front cover shows a wrapping cloth (*furoshiki*) by Kathleen Sunn.
The sashiko projects on the back cover are by the author.
Photographs by Katsuhiko Hidaka.

Distributed in the United States by Kodansha International/ USA Ltd., 114 Fifth Avenue, New York, New York 10011.
Published by Kodansha International Ltd., 17-14, Otowa 1-chome, Bunkyo-ku, Tokyo 112 and Kodansha International/ USA Ltd.
ISBN 4-7700-1436-8 (Japan)
First edition, 1990
Second printing, 1990
Library of Congrass Cataloging-in-Publication Data

Matsunaga, Karen Kim, 1958–
 Japanese country quilting: Sashiko pattarns and projects/ Karen Kim Matsunaga.
  p.   cm.
 ISBN 0-87011-936-2 (U.S.)
 1. Sashiko. 2. Quilting—Japan—Patterns. I. Title.
TT835.M389   1990
746.46—dc20

CONTENTS

Part Three: Projects

INTRODUCTION: What is Sashiko?

Sashiko is a simple running stitch worked in repeating or interlocking patterns through one or more layers of fabric. Typically, the patterns are executed in white cotton thread on indigo-dyed fabric. The traditional patterns readily lend themselves to modern decorative applications, such as purely decorative embroidery, but the stitching was originally designed for quilting together several layers of fabric for warmth and durability or for strengthening a single layer of fabric.

Like quilting in the West, sashiko is a humble craft with humble beginnings. It requires neither exotic silks nor years of apprenticeship to attain mastery. In former times, every household included at least one member who did sashiko stitching. With sashiko, torn garments were mended, dust cloths were stitched together, and aprons were created from threadbare fabrics. Today, while some rural households continue the traditional sashiko, most items decorated with the stitching are made in cottage industries for sale in tourist shops; these primarily decorative adaptations are very different from their functional forebears.

The Japanese have been doing sashiko for practical purposes since ancient times, when most people lived in houses made of wood and bamboo with thatched roofs and earthen or raised floors. The main room of these country houses contained a sunken hearth, which was at or near the center of the room. The Japanese family often encircled the hearth, which, as the home's only source of light and heat, became the center of family life and a symbol of hospitality. A hook of wood or metal was suspended above the square-shaped hearth and a kettle of water or a cooking pot was hung from it. The family gathered here to eat, to talk, and to sew. In this atmosphere of warmth and light, clothes were mended and stitched.

The fire in the hearth not only heated water and meals, but also was used to get the iron piping hot for sewing. Before electricity became widely available, the traditional iron, an iron wedge with a long wooden handle, was placed into the ashes to absorb the heat, then wiped clean before being used for pressing seams.

In those early days, clothes worn by the common people were

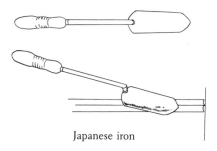

Japanese iron

7

made from homespun fabrics woven from the fibers of the paper mulberry, wisteria, hemp, and other bast-fiber plants. Fabric and garments were troublesome to make, so people developed ways to recycle fabric and extend the life of their clothes. Early efforts to conserve cloth can be seen in the life of the traditional kimono. From the initial construction of the kimono, there is no waste. Each bolt of fabric (averaging 14″ wide and 12 yards long) makes exactly one kimono. Since the kimono is constructed entirely of rectangular pieces that fit together like a jigsaw puzzle, not one scrap of fabric remains after the garment is completed.

Once the kimono of yore showed signs of wear, it began a long series of transformations. When it could no longer serve as one's Sunday best, the kimono was worn as everyday dress. The garment was later used as a sleeping gown or shortened to serve as an outdoor jacket. When further worn, the fabric from the gown or jacket was made into, say, an apron and a bag for use in gathering bamboo shoots. Finally, layers of fabric scraps were sashiko-quilted together into dust cloths, which were stored in the hollow of a wooden footstool for future use.

Another method of extending the life of a garment was to use a running stitch to hold layers of patches in place. Some examples of this sashiko from the 1800s hold together many layers of fabric positioned one atop the other to preserve a well-worn jacket or other favorite garment. Records show that this simple patchwork was done by both men and women.

Not only were scraps of fabric saved but lengths of thread were also collected for sashiko stitching. One of the drawers of the traditional wooden sewing box was often reserved for stray pieces of thread. Another drawer contained a slot at the top for inserting broken pins and needles.

The crude fabrics used in early times provided little relief from the cold. The same articles of clothing were worn in all seasons, and winters were often described by the number of layers people had to wear—for example, a "two-layer" winter or a particularly cold, "three-layer" winter. It was soon discovered that garments with stitched-in linings provided even better protection against the bitter cold.

It is no wonder, then, that some of the most beautiful examples of sashiko come from Tohoku, the northern region of Japan's main island, where snow covers the ground for half the year. During the long, harsh winters, when farmwork was discontinued, men and women prepared for the coming spring. Such winter tasks included transporting fertilizer, making charcoal, mending fishing nets, weaving, and sewing. The cold winter months forced people indoors where they could perfect their needlecrafts.

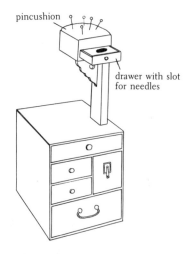

pincushion

drawer with slot for needles

Japanese sewing box

While northern residents continued to cultivate and weave linen for clothing, all cotton goods were produced abroad. In the 1300s and 1400s, virtually all of the cotton imported to Japan went to the nobility. In fact, one symbol of prosperity was an outfit made of cotton. A wealthy man was one who wore a long cotton kimono and a thin cotton handtowel (*tenugui*) that covered his head and cheeks.

But as large quantities of cotton began to appear on the market in the 1700s, cotton goods gradually became accessible to the common people. Once they discovered the absorbency, warmth, and texture of cotton, it became a highly desired commodity and attempts were made to cultivate it domestically. Cotton cultivation soon flourished in southern prefectures, but even after cotton became prevalent throughout most of Japan, it remained a treasure to the northern residents.

The cotton fabrics and thread that found their way to the snow country were considered precious goods. Sashiko was used extensively to conserve the limited supply of cotton in the north. One conservation method was the counted-thread technique of sashiko. Rather than weave a bolt of cloth entirely of cotton, long cotton threads were stitched through bolts of linen fabric. Warp and weft threads were counted and the cotton was handstitched at regular intervals. This lent the cloth strength and warmth with a minimal amount of cotton.

Sashiko was also used to extend the life of 100% cotton fabric. One example of this usage was found in the construction of tabi, or Japanese two-toed socks. Like the design of mittens, in which the thumb is separated from the other fingers, Japanese socks were split between the large toe and the other four toes. This design accommodated the thong in straw sandals and wooden clogs. The socks had to be sturdy and warm. Since outer footwear was not worn indoors, the bottom of the sock wore out easily. To forestall wear, the entire bottom surface was strengthened with sashiko. In the 1800s, as many as four layers of cotton flannel were sashiko-stitched together to form the sole. Today, tabi soles consist of one or two layers of starched heavy fabric.

By the 1800s, cotton was used in remote areas for such items as underwear, head coverings, and sashes—evidence that cotton fabric had become plentiful even in the north. The recycling and mending continued, but a new dimension was added: sashiko became valued for its decorative qualities as well as for its practicality. Traditional Japanese patterns and motifs were incorporated into sashiko stitching. Since cotton fabrics were softer and easier to sew than native linen and bast-fiber fabrics, more intricate designs became possible. Before marriage, young women might prepare ten work vests, enough to last a lifetime,

9

covered with fine sashiko stitching. Indeed, the ability to do sashiko well became an attribute of a good bride. Thus sashiko became entwined in the lives of Japan's rural people.

Weaving and sewing were an important part of life, as evinced by two traditional events still celebrated today. One, the yearly Tanabata festival, is based on a Chinese legend about the romance between the Weaving Maid, represented by the star Vega, and the Cow Herd, represented by the star Altair. The Weaving Maid worked at her loom day after day to weave the clouds and mists. One day, however, after falling in love with the Cow Herd, she neglected her weaving duties. Her father, in a rage, separated the lovers with the Milky Way and permitted his daughter to see the Cow Herd only once a year on the seventh day of the seventh month. Every year on that night, magpies make a bridge with their wings across the Milky Way so that the lovers may meet. The Weaving Maid is still honored on July 7 by Japanese girls who hope they can attain skill in weaving or other arts.

Another event demonstrating the value placed on needlework in Japan is the annual ceremony of *hari kuyo*. Once a year, bent and broken pins and needles are gathered from the household and taken to a local Shinto shrine. The needles and pins are inserted into large blocks of tofu or *konnyaku* (a gelatinous food). The original purpose of the ceremony was probably to give the sewing instruments a comfortable resting place, to enable a sewer to express appreciation for the necessary tools of his or her craft, and to pray for sewing skills in the coming year. This annual service exemplifies the spirit in which tools and fabrics were used.

Today, some country folk as well as the older generation throughout Japan continue to stitch dust cloths and aprons with sashiko, but you are more likely to see sashiko of a decorative nature in modern households, typically on such items as doorway curtains and table runners. Indeed sashiko has enjoyed a resurgence among young Japanese women in recent years as part of a nationwide revival of interest in traditional arts and crafts. As in centuries past, sashiko continues to provide an attractive, potentially functional accent to household items, clothing, and accessories.

Part

ONE

Tools & Techniques

Stitching the Design

The selection of fabric, thread, and stitch length will affect the look of any sashiko design. Although sashiko is a very simple stitch, its range of applications—whether quilting or embroidery—can be broadened by experimenting with these variables.

FABRIC

In Japan, sashiko is most commonly seen on indigo-dyed cotton fabric, the traditional favorite. Most of the antique sashiko garments that exist today are made of dark-indigo cotton with a light-blue cotton lining.

There were good reasons to use indigo-dyed cloth. Natural indigo dye contains natural ammonia that makes the fibers bug-resistant, and the indigo color becomes more beautiful with fading and age. Farmers once believed that clothes dyed in indigo would protect them from snakes in the field. Despite the selection of native vegetable dyes available to them, country folk often chose indigo to dye their cloth.

The intensity of the color is controlled by the number of immersions of the fabric in the indigo vat. The fabric can be dipped as many as twenty times, depending on the desired shade. In the past, there were some fifteen different names given to the subtle differences in shade. The lightest color was known as *kame-nozoki*, or "a peep into the (indigo) vat," while the deep blue-black popular with samurai warriors was dubbed *kachi-iro*, or "victory color."

Japanese indigo-dyed fabrics are available in the U.S. (see Appendix 1), but most come in the standard narrow width of fabric (14"–16") that evolved from the dimensions of the Chinese drawloom introduced to Japan in 500 A.D. A single bolt of this fabric, averaging 14" wide and 12 yards long, goes into making exactly one kimono or one obi sash, and indeed most Japanese sewing projects are geared to this narrow width. Instructions for the traditional projects in this book offer a choice of Japanese or Western widths—15", 36", 45", and 60".

In modern times, fabrics dyed with natural indigo are more difficult to obtain and there is less need to protect clothing from bug damage. In fact, the creative potential of sashiko broadens dramatically as new materials are introduced. Linen, silk, wool, synthetics, and blends are all suitable, as are all colors, whether solids or prints. Be sure to consider the use of the completed project in selecting a fabric. A delicate silk requiring dry-cleaning, for example, is not the best choice for a bag that will undergo heavy use.

Fabrics made specifically for needlework projects are also suitable. Sashiko patterns composed of straight lines that meet at right angles (e.g., Blossoms, Hydrangea, Measuring Boxes, Mountains, Persimmon Flower, Stone Pavement, Sun Symbol, and "Ten" Pattern) can be stitched on evenweave cotton and linen fabric designed for counted-thread embroidery. The evenweave fabrics have an equal number of warp and weft threads per square inch and come in various degrees of coarseness ranging from 11 threads per inch to 36 threads per inch. To use, count threads as you stitch. For example, stitch across three threads for each movement of the needle. This method, which was employed in the original sashiko of ancient times, is especially suited to such patterns as Arrow Feathers 3, Blossoms, Hydrangea, Mountains, Measuring Boxes, and Persimmon Flower.

The light "fleece" weight of (polyester) batting is recommended for quilted projects, as it is easier to maintain the sashiko pattern on both front and back sides of the project when the total bulk of fabric and batting is thinner. On quilts (and other lined projects) you may wish to use sashiko as a decorative embroidery stitch that goes through only the top layer of fabric; after the layers are assembled, more sashiko can be stitched through all layers as a quilting stitch.

If the seemingly infinite choice of materials seems overwhelming, beginners may want to start with the classic combination of indigo-blue cotton or cotton-blend fabric with white cotton thread. The simplicity and warmth of the blue and white has timeless appeal. As with all fine sewing, prewash and iron the fabric before starting any sashiko project.

THREAD

Traditional sashiko thread is 100% cotton and has a stringlike quality. See Appendix 1 for U.S. suppliers of sashiko thread. Inexpensive crochet thread is probably the closest equivalent in the West. Pearl cotton #5 and four strands of embroidery floss are also comparable.

As a general rule, when deciding on the kind of thread to use, match the fiber content of the thread to the fiber content of the cloth. For example, crochet thread, embroidery floss, and pearl cotton are suitable for cotton and cotton-blend fabrics. But don't be a slave to this rule. After all, sashiko was first stitched with cotton thread on linen fabric.

Other threads you can use include silk embroidery floss, pearl cotton #3 and #8 (commonly sold in three weights—#3, #5, and #8, #3 being the thickest), flower threads, and blending filaments (gold, silver, and other metallics).

Tiny stitches require finer thread while large stitches lend themselves to heavier thread or a multistrand combination of threads. Embroidery floss can be separated into strands to vary the weight of the stitching. Three or four strands can be used for delicate stitches; all six strands combined yields bolder stitches. Use one or two strands of the other threads noted above, depending on the weight of the fabric and the length of the stitches. Try some sample stitches on a scrap piece of fabric and adjust the weight or ply of the thread to achieve the effect you desire.

Blending filaments are combined with other threads and then stitched as if one strand. For example, two strands of gold thread work nicely with two strands of embroidery floss. Each blending filament must be threaded in a special way to prevent it from fraying and breaking as you stitch. Form a small loop in the blending filament and thread the loop through the needle. Then bring the needle point through the loop and pull, tightening the loop around the eye of the needle. This anchors the filament to the needle. Finally, thread the needle with any other type of thread to be used.

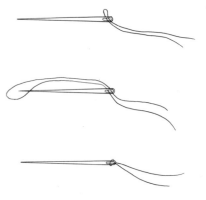

Threading a blending filament

For all types of thread, cut a 20″ piece for stitching. If the strand is too short, you will have to rethread your needle often. If the strand is too long, it will tangle and fray. As my grandmother warned, "Only a greenhorn uses a long thread!"

Here is a method the Japanese use to prevent the thread from twisting around itself: Before threading the needle, hold the length of thread taut by wrapping each end around the middle finger of each hand. Give the thread two snaps with the thumb.

NEEDLES

Select a needle type and size that suits the fabric and thread and that feels comfortable when you do a running stitch. If it is difficult to pull the needle through the fabric, and the thread frays easily, the needle may be too small. If the stitching leaves holes in the fabric, the needle may be too large. Needles are sold by number—the lower the number, the longer and thicker the needle. Among readily available needles suitable for sashiko are the following:

Embroidery or crewel needles have long eyes that accommodate a number of strands of floss. Their sharp points are good for stitching cotton, silk, and wool fabric. **Tapestry needles** have large eyes and blunt points that do not damage coarsely woven fabric. Use these needles when sewing on linen and evenweave fabrics. **Quilting needles** have round eyes and are suited to doing sashiko as a quilting stitch through cotton fabric and batting layers.

Needles made specifically for sashiko are manufactured in Japan and available in the U.S. through the suppliers listed in Appendix 1. Typically, one package contains four different lengths (and widths) of needles with various eye sizes. There is no pressing need to acquire Japanese needles, however, as the Western needles noted above are perfectly suitable for sashiko stitching.

THIMBLES

Unlike the cap-shaped thimbles of the West, the Japanese thimble is a ring of leather or metal worn on the middle finger of the sewing hand between the first and second joints. A thimble isn't really necessary for sashiko unless you are sewing through many layers of fabric or you are more comfortable using one when handsewing a running stitch. Feel free to substitute a Western thimble.

JAPANESE HANDSEWING

"Moving needle" (*unshin*) is the name of the Japanese technique for sewing the basic running stitch. The eye of the needle is placed perpendicular to the Japanese thimble (worn on the middle finger), with the tip of the needle grasped by the thumb and forefinger. This position may seem awkward to the Western tailor, but it feels natural to those who sew kimonos.

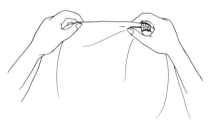

"Moving needle" technique

Another distinguishing feature of this technique is that the threaded needle is only occasionally pulled through the fabric. By manipulating the cloth with the left hand in a back and forth motion, and by alternating the pressure of the thumb and forefinger of the right hand on the needle, the needle is propelled forward through the fabric as it pushes against the thimble. This fluid motion, when mastered, is perfect for sewing garments, like the kimono, that are constructed mostly of straight seams. It is also ideal for stitching the straight lines of sashiko patterns.

Warm-up exercises in traditional Japanese sewing classes consist of sewing rows of running stitches. Once a week, students count the number of stitches they can do in a one-minute period, checking not only for quantity, but for evenness and straightness of the seam as well. Not long ago, learning the "moving needle" technique was a grade school requirement for both girls and boys in Japan.

SASHIKO NEEDLEWORK

The running stitch is the only stitch used for sashiko. The number of stitches per inch depends on the type of fabric, the number of fabric layers, and the type of thread used. As a general rule, use larger stitches for heavy fabrics and heavy thread and smaller stitches for fine fabrics and fine thread. For example, sewing with two strands of crochet thread will result in fewer (large) stitches per inch while using three strands of embroidery floss will result in more (delicate) stitches per inch.

The fine stitching on the Wrapping Cloth project (see front cover) is about 8 stitches per inch, while the Triangle Bag (see back cover) is decorated with 6 stitches per inch. In general, traditional sashiko ranges in scale from 4 to 8 stitches per inch.

Begin sashiko stitches with a knot or with two to three overlap stitches. To sew overlap stitches, begin by making a few stitches in the opposite direction of the intended stitching line. Then backtrack over the original stitches, piercing the thread while sewing. The fibers of the thread interlock and the overlap stitches stay put even with handling and repeated washings. The overlap method is neater and best for projects that will be seen from both sides, like the Doorway Curtain and the Wrapping Cloth.

Keep the stitches as uniform in length as possible. If the number of stitches in each segment of the patterns is equal, the intersecting points and overall design will be neat and uniform. Some Japanese stress that individual stitches should never cross one another. Thus, where two or more lines of stitching intersect, as in the Hemp Leaf pattern, the stitches form a multipetalled "flower" with an unstitched "hole" in the center. Nevertheless, since numerous examples of old and modern sashiko stitched in Japan show no concern for this fine point, you needn't worry about stitching perfect flowers at intersections, unless you like the challenge.

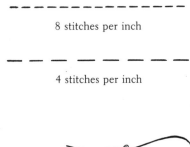

8 stitches per inch

4 stitches per inch

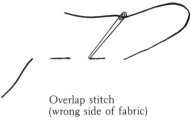

Overlap stitch
(wrong side of fabric)

"Flower" intersections

Each segment has an equal number of stitches.

Drawing and Transferring the Design

Just as the selection of thread and fabric influences the finished sashiko project, so do the size and placement of the design on the project. This section describes the tools and method used to produce sashiko patterns and to transfer them onto the fabric.

Drawing the designs on paper enables experimentation and familiarization with the sashiko motifs before making the considerable time investment of stitching with needle and thread. The right tools will make this step more pleasant, so gather them together and then start. Transferring the design onto the fabric correctly will make the stitching go more smoothly.

TOOLS

TEMPLATES: Since many sashiko patterns are composed of interlocking circles or semicircles, it is a good investment to buy a plastic template of various-sized circles. Such templates can be purchased at art supply and stationery stores. Alternatively, make your own templates with a compass and cardboard or plastic.

Some patterns (e.g., Plum Blossom and Waves 2) require special templates that you must make yourself. Draw the design on template plastic (sold in quilting shops), cardboard, or plastic from coffee-can lids. Cut the shapes out with scissors or with an X-acto type knife.

RULER: Any kind of straight-edged ruler can be used for drawing and transferring sashiko designs. However, a clear quilters' ruler is the ideal tool for measuring and drawing lines. The grid markings on the quilters' ruler make measuring a simple task, and the transparency allows you to see previous markings beneath the ruler, enabling greater accuracy. This type of ruler can be purchased at art supply, craft, or fabric shops.

PROTRACTOR: A protractor is needed for drawing the angles in the Chrysanthemum and both Folding Fans patterns.

GRAPH PAPER: The use of graph paper will save you much time and frustration when drafting the sashiko patterns. Most of the patterns can be drawn on a ¼″ grid—that is, graph paper that has sixteen blocks to the square inch. Vellumlike graph paper (sold under such brand names as Clear Print) is recommended. This sturdy paper does not tear easily under the pressure of the tracing wheel when you transfer designs onto fabric. Therefore, a pattern can be reused many times.

Tablets of $8\frac{1}{2}$" × 11" (letter size) graph paper are available at stationery shops or drugstores, and larger sheets (e.g., 2' × 3') can be purchased at art supply stores. The large sheets are more versatile since most projects are larger than letter-size paper. If big sheets of graph paper are not available, tape smaller sheets together until you have the appropriate size for your project.

Some patterns—for example, Cypress Fence 2, Linked Diamonds, and Silk Weave 2—are most easily drawn on paper with an isometric grid. This triangular-grid paper is carried by well-stocked art supply stores. (The Clear Print brand comes in 2' × 3' sheets.)

Draw on the graph paper with pencil the first time. When you are satisfied with the pattern, you may wish to go over the lines with a felt-tip pen to prevent eye strain and to enable reuse of the pattern.

TRACING PAPER: Use dressmakers' tracing paper (opaque paper with a chalklike coating on one side) to transfer the pattern drawing to the fabric. Particularly handy is a single package containing various colors of paper, which may be purchased at fabric shops. Follow the manufacturer's instructions on the package for best results. Make sure the markings are washable before you begin transferring your design onto the fabric. Use a tracing wheel or empty ball-point pen with the paper when transferring the pattern to the fabric.

SCORING TOOL: Dressmakers in Japan use a scoring tool made of bone, ivory, or plastic instead of a tracing wheel and tracing paper. The tool, called a *hera*, is a simple, bladelike object that averages 6" in length. It has a thin, slightly curved edge for scoring fabric. When the proper amount of pressure is applied, the *hera* leaves an indented line in cotton and silk fabrics that does not disappear until the cloth is washed. In this way, the tool is used to make small dashlike marks where tailor tacks would be used in the West. For sashiko, the *hera* is used to transfer the pattern from the graph paper to the cloth, with tracing paper between the two layers. See Appendix 1 for U.S. suppliers.

marking edge

Hera (scoring tool)

You may prefer using a Western-style tracing wheel and tracing paper (see above), which serve the same purpose.

WRITING INSTRUMENTS: There are many types of drawing instruments suitable for touching up the transferred pattern on the cloth. Select a writing instrument that leaves clear but washable lines. Lines drawn with dressmakers' chalk tend to smear and rub off as you stitch, requiring frequent (and frustrating) redrawing. On the other hand, ball-point pens and some markers leave undesirable permanent lines.

One solution is to use colored pencils, many of which are suitable for drawing on fabric. Use light blue and yellow pencils for dark fabrics and pink or light green for light-colored fabrics. The lines stay put through the stitching but wash out well. Another option is to use water-soluble markers sold in fabric shops. The marks made with these pens disappear in plain water. As with all marking instruments, test for washability on a scrap of the fabric before use.

METHOD

Draw the project to scale on graph paper if it is difficult to visualize the desired finished piece. You might use a ¼″ grid paper with each block representing 1″ or more, depending on the size of the project. Now sketch in the outlines of the areas you wish to cover with sashiko—anywhere from a single spot to the entire surface. Adjust the area until you are satisfied that it suits the project use, project size, pattern(s) selected, and choice of fabric and thread.

Now, on a different piece of graph paper, draw the pattern area outlines to their actual size. Fill in the area with the sashiko pattern selected, using the appropriate drawing tools.

Place the drawing on the cut-out fabric to make sure it is the appropriate size, design, and placement for the project. If necessary, redraw the pattern in different sizes and arrangements until you are satisfied with it.

Select a color of tracing paper that resembles the fabric color but contrasts sufficiently to avoid eye strain. Always pretest the tracing-paper markings for washability.

Lay the fabric right-side up on a flat surface. Place hard, thick cardboard under the fabric. The cardboard will give a little under the pressure of a tracing wheel or empty ballpoint pen, resulting in a sharp line on the fabric. Position the graph-paper drawing over the fabric and pin it in place so it does not slip. Carefully insert the tracing paper between the drawing and the fabric.

Now, trace over the pattern lines, putting enough pressure on the tracing wheel or pen so that the design transfers to the cloth. Avoid going over a line more than once or you will get a double image. A line that is too light can be darkened manually by drawing directly on the fabric with a colored pencil or nonpermanent fabric marker after the entire pattern has been transferred.

Work through the design systematically to ensure that every line is transferred. For example, start at one edge of the drawing and transfer all the horizontal lines, then the vertical lines, then the diagonal lines, and finally the curves. When you are done, remove the drawing and tracing paper and examine the markings on the fabric. Redraw (directly on the fabric) any sections that are too light or that were missed. You may have to redraw lines periodically while stitching since they tend to fade as the cloth is handled.

DESIGNING WITH SASHIKO
Placement of sashiko designs on a cloth surface may be determined primarily by functional concerns. A farmer's jacket may bear sashiko stitching just on the shoulder areas to prevent wear from carrying heavy loads. A wrapping cloth typically is reinforced with sashiko at the four corners, which are frequently tied and untied, and in the center, where the load is placed.

Sashiko placement may also be determined by aesthetic concerns. One good source of ideas for designing with sashiko is classic kimono design. The following are a few of the basic principles of kimono design that may be applied to sashiko to achieve a Japanese look.

"Shoulders and hem" is a kimono design consisting of decoration (embroidery, dyeing, etc.) at the shoulder and at the hem, with the expanse between left free of embellishment. This use of blank space, a common theme in Japanese design, is a boon to the sashiko worker, as it conserves effort while enhancing the design. Pay attention to the lines and shapes created by the blank (unstitched) areas of your sashiko project. Try placing the

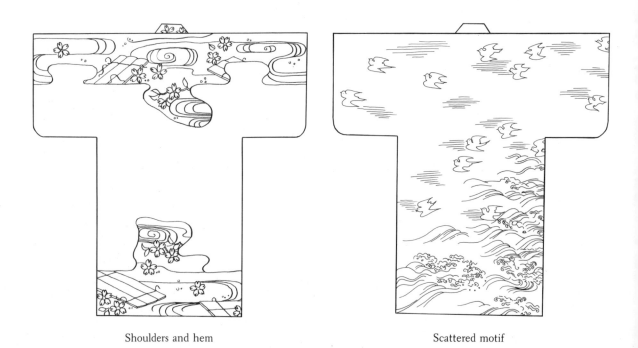

Shoulders and hem   Scattered motif

stitching at just the top and bottom edges of the item, avoiding exact symmetry.

Similarly, a large area of undecorated space characterizes the "scattered motif" composition. In this kimono design, several motifs are scattered over the entire surface of the kimono with lots of open space between them. A free, yet not haphazard, distribution of patterns is considered more elegant. A balance is obtained by carefully selecting the number and size of a motif.

The use of a few large motifs grouped in clusters is another common kimono design. Try isolating a single element of a sashiko design—say, a fan from Folding Fans—and enlarging it. Use it as is, or as an outline to be filled in with other sashiko patterns. You can also use the isolated motif in combination with the same element magnified to different sizes. Some of the other sashiko patterns that lend themselves to this technique are Pine Bark (enlarged on the Doorway Curtain project), Seven Treasures (enlarged on the Wrapping Cloth project), Sun Symbol, and Waves 1.

In the "differing halves" composition, the right and left halves of a kimono are of different fabrics, patterns, or colors. For sashiko projects, you might stitch half of the decorated surface with one pattern and the other half with a different pattern (or leave it unstitched). Another possibility is to stitch the same pattern in different colors on each half of the decorated space.

A variation on this composition is a large-squared checkerboard of two (or more) different fabrics, patterns, or colors. One

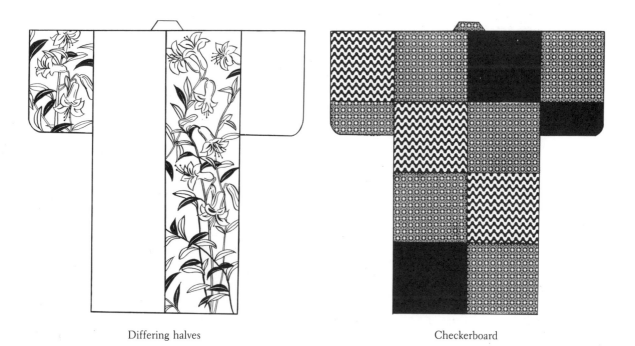

Differing halves   Checkerboard

way to apply this composition is to sashiko-stitch with colored thread in alternate squares and use plain fabric that matches the thread for the remaining squares.

The kimono surface may also be divided into unequal areas with a straight diagonal line or a large zigzag line called a "lightning bolt." The resulting subdivisions are given different decorative treatment. The basic unit of the Pine Bark pattern is similarly used to divide space into sub-areas containing different patterns (see the Doorway Curtain project). The Japanese love of diagonal division of space is seen in many arts—lacquerware, ceramics, and filmmaking, to name a few.

Two other design principles to keep in mind are asymmetry and suggestion. Symmetrical arrangements never had lasting popularity in Japan. Even a "square" floor cushion or wrapping cloth is not perfectly square. (See the dimensions for these two projects—both are actually squarish rectangles.) Running a pattern off the edge of the fabric, as if to suggest its continuation, or ending a pattern "abruptly" before reaching a natural stopping point (a seam, stitched outline, etc.) are common design techniques that call on the imagination to fill in the rest of the picture.

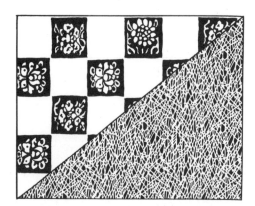

Diagonal line

Lightning bolt

Pine Bark outline

Part

TWO

Patterns

Sashiko patterns are simple, geometric designs born of Japan's long heritage of decorative arts. Far from being the exclusive property of needleworkers, many of the sashiko patterns in use today may be seen on pieces of fine art as well as on textiles, ceramics, musical instruments, and even weapons.

Geometric designs of the sort basic to many sashiko patterns existed in Japan from the earliest times. The sashiko patterns Crossed Cords and Fish Scales, for example, are identical to designs that have been found on primitive ceramic wares.

As different cultures were introduced to Japan, the decorative palette expanded. Patterns of native origin were combined with those from China and Korea, which in turn had been influenced by Greece, the Middle East, and India. The introduction of Buddhism, too, brought an influx of new art and architecture. Sashiko motifs originating in Buddhist sculpture and scrolls include Hemp Leaf, Pampas Grass, Silk Weave 1, and Waves 1.

In time, because of such factors as the patronage of wealthy warlords and aristocrats, 250 years of isolation from the world (1600–1865), and the people's aesthetic sensibility, a native Japanese style emerged. Foreign influences were absorbed and transformed, not merely imitated. Fashions changed with the times, but the delight Japanese took in nature and seasonal changes remained a constant through the centuries. Flowers, grasses, and trees associated with specific seasons became popular motifs. Just as a poetic reference to cherry blossoms conjured up images of spring, simple shapes and motifs became stylized seasonal symbols that were instantly recognized by the Japanese people. A few arcs represented pampas grass and an arrangement of semicircles became plovers in flight—both symbols of autumn.

The natural beauty of simple things—the texture of a basket, the curve of a branch—inspired artists and craftspeople as they developed motifs to decorate religious and everyday objects. Even the simplest patterns were given charming names taken from common items they resembled. Rising Steam and Woven Bamboo are two such examples.

Another constant in the Japanese philosophy of ornamentation was the belief that, although function was of primary consideration when designing an object, decoration was an integral part of that design. The folk-craft movement that began in the early 1900s revolved around this point. The handmade functional objects that emerged directly from the daily needs of the common people could be uncommonly beautiful. This art of the country people was named *mingei*, or folk crafts. Sashiko is one of these folk crafts where design and function are inseparable.

Starting in the eighth century, the patronage of court nobles and wealthy citizens spurred artists to develop elaborate embroidery techniques and patterns for textiles using expensive, exotic materials. In contrast to full-time artists, farmers and fishermen could work on their garments only during their spare time. Out of necessity the country people selected patterns for their ability to strengthen the fabric or garment. Since cloth of native plant fibers was coarse and difficult to sew, simple lines and angles formed the basis of decoration. Some of the oldest sashiko patterns composed of simple lines are Measuring Boxes, Mountains, and Persimmon Flower.

When cotton fabrics became available, the softness of the material allowed for the stitching of more complex decorative patterns without having to sacrifice the reinforcing qualities of sashiko. In modern Japan, with less concern about conserving fabric and the availability of diverse fibers and fabrics, sashiko is looked upon more as a decorative craft.

Let your imagination be your guide in designing with sashiko. The fifty-two patterns presented here can be modified or applied to other media. Try designing your own repeating pattern featuring a favorite motif—a maple leaf, American Indian pattern, or company logo. Experiment with sashiko on paper, leather, knits, or other stitchable surfaces. The sashiko patterns may be used as spot or all-over designs on any flat surface in need of embellishment.

* * *

Each of the following patterns includes instructions for drawing and stitching the pattern. The patterns can be drawn on graph paper with a ¼″ square grid or, where indicated, graph paper with a triangular grid.

While there is often a variety of stitching sequences possible, an attempt has been made to present the most efficient order for stitching each design. Begin at the lowest circled number (that is, ①) and then follow the path indicated by arrows. Stitch all the lines or curves that go in the described direction before continuing to the next circled number. Although starting and ending points are indicated by knots in the illustrations, feel free to use any method to begin and end a line of stitches. Curved arrows indicate the thread passing along the wrong side of the fabric.

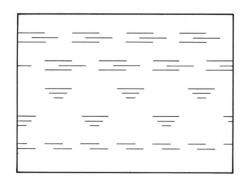

Arrow Feathers 1 (*yabane*)

These three versions of the Arrow Feathers pattern are easy to draw and stitch. Any of the three makes an attractive all-over design (see the Doorway Curtain for a stitched example), or modify the third version to create a bold outline stitch (Fig. *a*). The center circle of the Wrapping Cloth is outlined with this bold stitch.

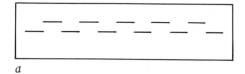

a

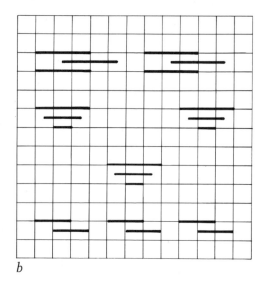

b

To draw (Fig. *b*): Use the grid on graph paper to draw evenly spaced rows of stitches.

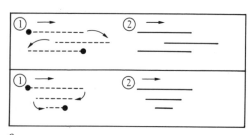

c

To stitch:

METHOD 1 (Fig. *c*): Stitch each *set* of lines before proceeding to the next set. Use this method when the sets of lines are spaced far apart.

METHOD 2 (Fig. *d*): Stitch each horizontal line of stitching across the entire design area before beginning the next row. Use this method when the sets of lines are close together or when using the counted-thread technique.

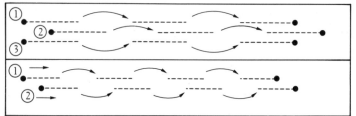

d

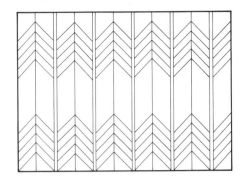

Arrow Feathers 2 (*yabane*)

The bow and arrow was a weapon of war in ancient Japan, with warriors becoming proficient in its use even on horseback. In the past, as well as today, archery is practiced as part of Zen training. This pattern of stylized arrow feathers is easy to draw and stitch.

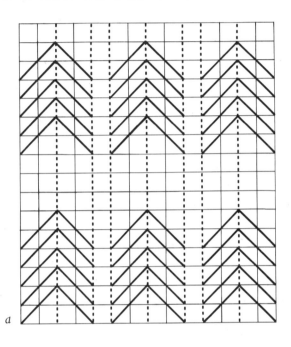

a

To draw: Draw vertical lines (dotted lines in Fig. *a*) spaced as shown: separated by 2 blocks, then 2 blocks, then 1 block. The number of spaces (2–2–1) between lines repeats. Next, draw short diagonal lines to form a zigzag pattern between the vertical lines, leaving the one-block column blank.

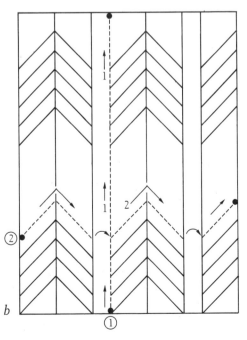

b

To stitch: First stitch all the vertical lines (1 in Fig. *b*). Then stitch the zigzag lines (2).

27

Arrow Feathers 3 (*yabane*)

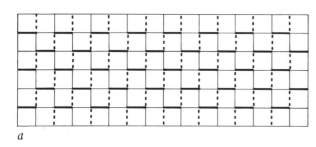

a

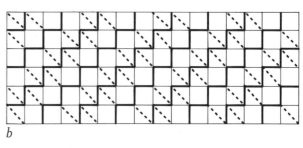

b

To draw: Draw horizontal dashed lines (solid lines in Fig. *a*), making the dashes and spaces equal in length (1 block long in this example). Next, draw vertical dashed lines in the same manner (dotted lines in Fig. *a*) to form zigzag lines. Finally, draw short diagonal lines, staggering them as shown (dotted lines in Fig. *b*).

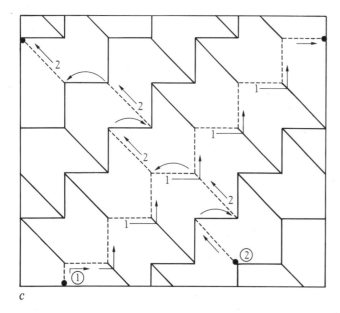

c

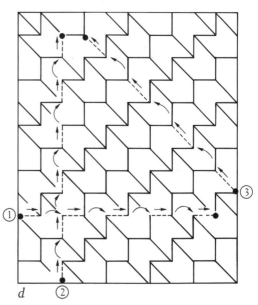

d

To stitch:

REGULAR METHOD (Fig. *c*): Stitch the zigzag lines (1) and then the short diagonal lines (2). Pass the thread behind the fabric between segments (curved arrows in illustration).

COUNTED-THREAD METHOD (Fig. *d*): First count the horizontal threads and stitch at equal intervals (1). For example, stitch over and under every five threads. Then count the vertical threads and stitch at equal intervals to form stairlike zigzag lines (2). Finally, fill in the diagonal lines to complete the pattern (3).

28

Bamboo (*take*)

The bamboo is an important plant in Japan since almost every part of it is used. The leaves keep rice balls fresh on long journeys, the stalk is made into utensils, vases, and musical instruments, and the shoots are a delicacy in Japanese cuisine. Because the plant grows tall and straight, bending yet rarely breaking even under heavy snow or in strong winds, it symbolizes endurance and perseverance. See the Wrapping Cloth project for an example of Bamboo used as a spot motif (among the pampas grass).

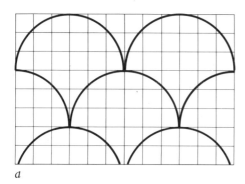

a

To draw: Draw rows of semicircles (Fig. *a*), using a circle template. Make a single template for the three bamboo leaves and trace it within the semicircles (dotted lines in Fig. *b*). You may wish to leave some semicircles blank.

b

c

To stitch (Fig. *c*): Stitch each row of semicircles (1). Stitch the outline of the 3 bamboo leaves (2). Stitch the leaf ribs (3, 4, 5).

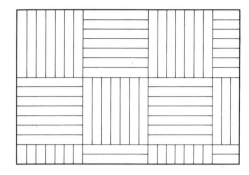

Basketweave

This original design created by Pam Jaasko was inspired by a Japanese fence pattern.

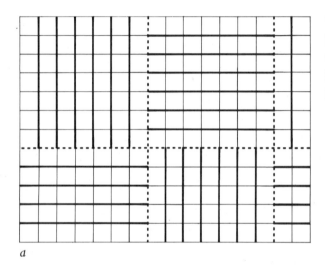

a

To draw (Fig. *a*): Divide the area into squares 7 blocks wide and 7 blocks tall (dotted lines). Then, within each block, draw 6 lines to divide each block into 7 stripes. Stripes in adjacent blocks should run in different directions—horizontal or vertical.

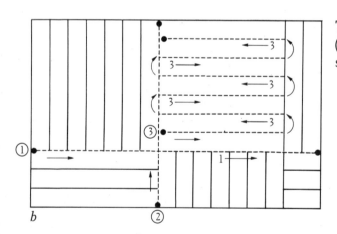

b

To stitch (Fig. *b*): Stitch the long horizontal lines (1) and then the long vertical lines (2). Finally, stitch the lines within each block (3).

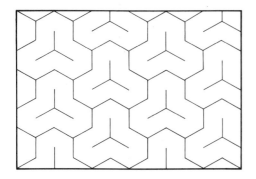

Bishamon 1 (*Bishamon*)

Bishamon is one of the seven gods of good fortune and the patron god of doctors, soldiers, and priests. This pattern is taken from the design that appears on Bishamon's armor and helmet. The pattern is a variation of the tortoise shell motif, another auspicious symbol in Japan. This sashiko pattern has numerous knots and is one of the more complicated designs to draw and stitch.

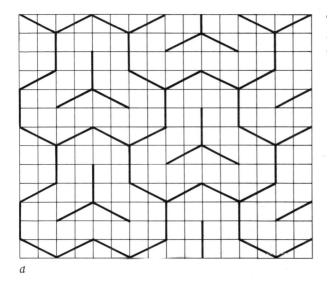

a

To draw (Fig. *a*): There is no simple way to draw this pattern. Begin at a corner point and count the blocks as you go.

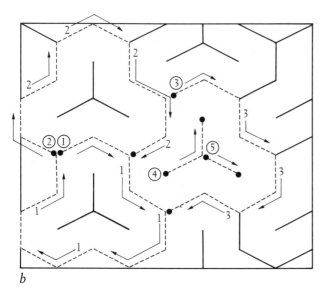

b

To stitch (Fig. *b*): First stitch each medallion separately (1, 2, 3). Then stitch the upside-down **Y** shape (4, 5).

Bishamon 2 (*Bishamon kikko*)

This pattern is one of the more difficult to draw and stitch. It requires many knots, so it is best used for projects that will be lined. See the Doorway Curtain for a stitched example of this pattern.

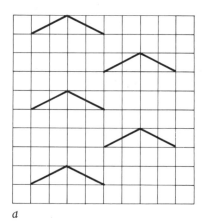

a

To draw: First draw diagonal lines to form wide angles (Fig. *a*). Count the blocks to position each set of lines. Then draw diagonal lines (dotted lines in Fig. *b*). Next draw short, vertical segments (Fig. *c*). Finally, draw short equal-length segments to form the upside-down **Y** shapes. (Use of a protractor to measure the 120° angles may help.)

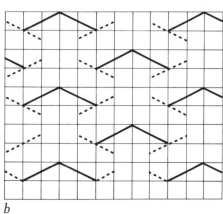

b

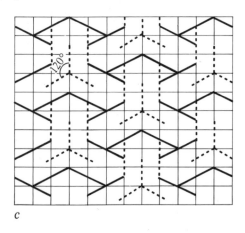

c

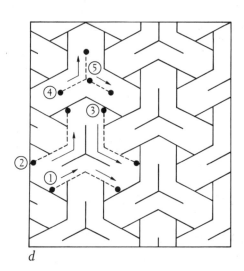

d

To stitch: Stitch each set of angles in any sequence. The numbered steps in Fig. *d* show one possibility.

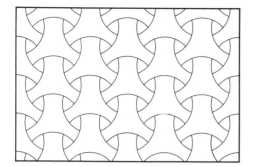

Bishamon 3 (*maru Bishamon*)

This pattern of interlocking circles requires a lot of knots.

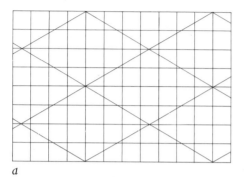

a

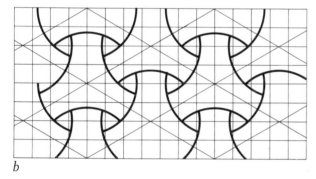

b

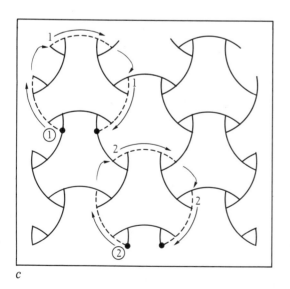

c

To draw: Lightly draw in diamond shapes (Fig. *a*). Each diamond should be comprised of two equilateral triangles. These lines will be guidelines, not part of the finished pattern. Next use a circle template, calculating the diameter of the circle with this ratio:

$$\frac{5}{7} = \frac{\text{length of triangle side}}{\text{diameter of circle}}$$

Another way to calculate the diameter is to divide the length of a triangle side by .71. Some examples are:

Triangle Side	Diameter
1″	1⅜″
2″	2¾″
2½″	3½″

Position the circle template with its center over the intersecting points of the diamond shapes. (On purchased templates, the quarter points of the circles are marked, so the template can be easily aligned using the grid and diamond shapes as guides.) Draw incomplete circles using the circle template (Fig. *b*).

To stitch: Stitch each circle in turn (Fig. *c*), passing the thread to the back of the fabric at the blank spaces (curved arrows in illustration).

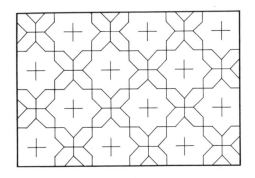

Blossoms (*juji hanazashi*)

The counted-thread method is used to stitch this design, so select an evenweave fabric. Draw the design on paper first even though the pattern will not be transferred onto the fabric. Drawing the design will familiarize you with the pattern, and your sketch will serve as a handy guide for stitching.

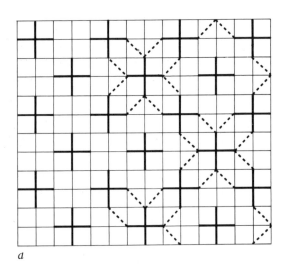

a

To draw (Fig. *a*): Draw evenly distributed plus signs (+). Then, connect the ends of the plus signs with diagonal lines.

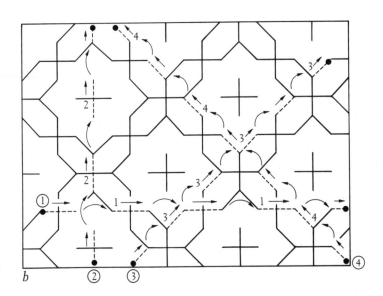

b

To stitch (Fig. *b*): Decide on the number of threads to be stitched for each segment. Each space and line represents an equal number of threads. For example, take a stitch every three threads of the fabric. In order, stitch the horizontal lines (1), then the vertical lines (2), and finally the diagonal lines (3, 4).

34

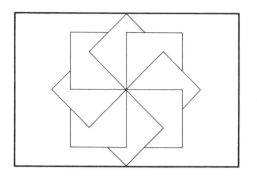

Cartwheel (*ishi-guruma*)

Ishi-guruma, the name of this pattern, literally means "stone cart." The design represents one of the wheels of a low, sturdy, four-wheeled cart that was used to transport stones in former times. This pattern may be repeated or used alone (enclosed in a circle or square) as a crest.

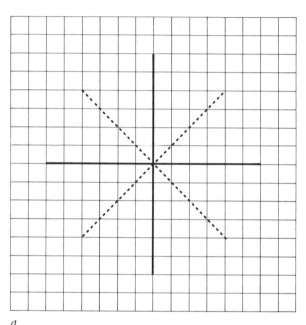

a

To draw: Draw a plus sign (solid lines in Fig. *a*). In this example, the line segments are each 12 blocks long. Draw another, slightly smaller plus sign at a 45° angle to the first (dotted lines). In this example, the lines of the smaller plus sign extend through the diagonals of 8 blocks. Next, draw lines (dotted lines in Fig. *b*) that radiate at a 90° angle from the ends of the plus sign spokes. The lines radiating from the first plus sign are 6 blocks long; the lines radiating from the second plus sign go through the diagonals of 4 blocks. Finally, draw lines that radiate at a 90° angle from the dotted lines that were just drawn.

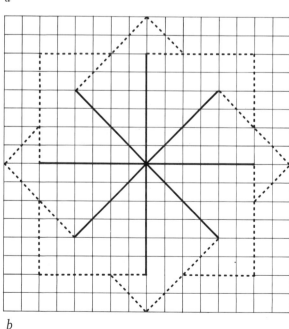

b

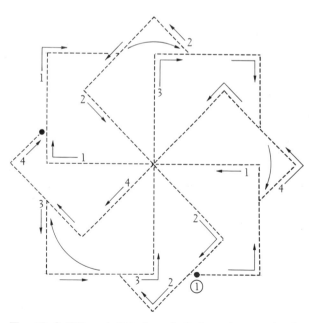

To stitch (Fig. *c*): Stitch each **S** shape in turn (1–4).

Chrysanthemum (*kiku*)

The chrysanthemum, an autumn flower, is highly prized in Japan. A chrysanthemum-viewing festival called the Feast of Happiness is held on September 9 in some parts of Japan, and the emperor's crest features a sixteen-petal chrysanthemum. In sashiko, a stylized version of the flower can be easily drawn and stitched. A 90° section of the pattern may be used to fill corners attractively. See the Wrapping Cloth and Doorway Curtain projects for stitched examples of this pattern.

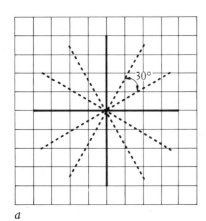

a

To draw: Begin by drawing two crossing lines of equal length at right angles (Fig. *a*). Use a protractor to divide each right angle into three equal parts (each part is 30°). Use a straightedge to draw segments of equal length to form the "spokes." Finally, using a circle template whose diameter matches the distance between the petal "spokes," connect each spoke with a semicircle (Fig. *b*). For example, if each spoke is 1″ long, the semicircle will have a diameter of ½″.

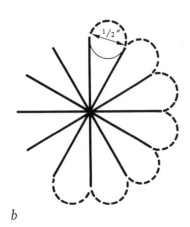

b

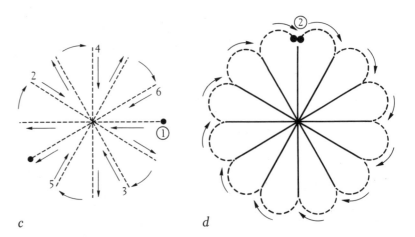

c   *d*

To stitch: First stitch all the spokes (Fig. *c*). Then stitch around the petal tips (Fig. *d*).

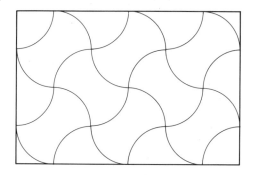

Counterweights (*fundo tsunagi*)

This pattern depicts connected scale counterweights. These counterweights are one of the standard-shape weights used with traditional Japanese scales.

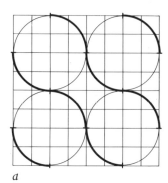

a

To draw: Begin by lightly drawing rows of circles, darkening only the arcs between quarter points (Fig. *a*). This results in the first set of wavy lines. Complete the second set of wavy lines by adding overlapping circles and darkening the arcs between their quarter points, shown as dotted wavy lines in Fig. *b*.

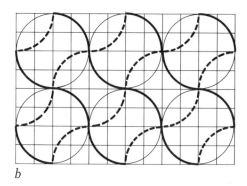

b

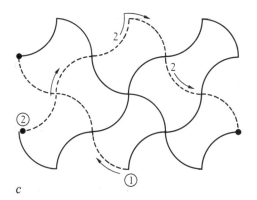

c

To stitch (Fig. *c*): Stitch all the wavy lines running in one direction (1). Then stitch all the wavy lines in the other direction. You can reduce the number of knots by turning the corner at the end of a row of stitching and continuing down a perpendicular line of stitching (2).

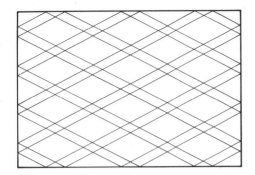

Crossed Cords (*tasuki*)

This simple design, found on prehistoric Japanese ceramics, is one of the oldest decorative patterns in Japan. The design was named *tasuki* after a narrow cord used to tie kimono sleeves up out of the way. When properly tied, this long cord forms an **X** across the wearer's back. Waitresses in traditional restaurants as well as fencers and festival participants still use these handy cords. This is one of the simplest patterns to draw and stitch and requires very few knots.

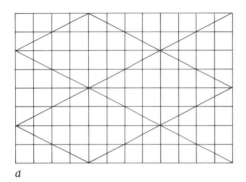

a

To draw: Lightly draw parallel diagonal lines to form diamond shapes (Fig. *a*). These lines will be guidelines, not part of the pattern. Next, draw parallel lines above and below the guidelines, keeping them equidistant from the guidelines (Fig. *b*). The dotted lines and heavy lines illustrate parallel lines above and below the guidelines.

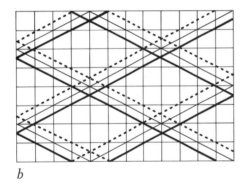

b

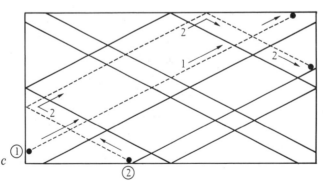

c

To stitch (Fig. *c*): Stitch each long straight line in turn (1). Alternatively, to reduce the number of knots, turn the corner at the end of a row of stitching and continue on (2).

Cypress Fence 1 (*higaki*)

This pattern represents a fence made of interwoven cypress strips. This wickerwork pattern is also used in garden fences made of woven bamboo. Cypress Fence 1 is one of the easiest patterns to draw and stitch.

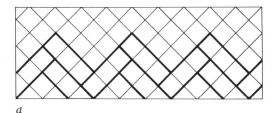

a

To draw (Fig. *a*): Draw the design on graph paper turned 45° so the lines run diagonally. Begin at a corner point and count the blocks as you draw.

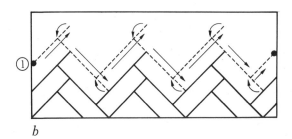

b

To stitch (Fig. *b*): Begin at one edge and stitch straight, short segments in a zigzag manner (Fig. *a*). In order to do this, stitch to the end of a segment, pass the thread to the back of the fabric (curved arrows in the illustration), and start the next perpendicular segment.

Cypress Fence 2 (*higaki*)

Use a triangular grid (isometric graph paper) to draw this variation on the basic Cypress Fence pattern.

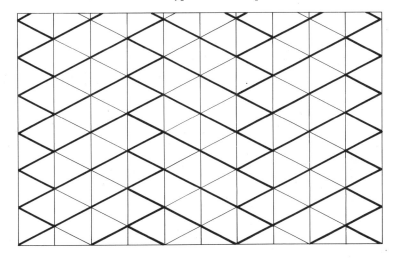

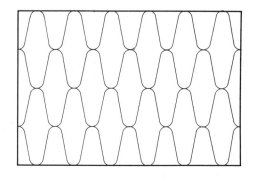

Fishing Net (*amime*)

This popular pattern appears on ceramic dishes and lacquerware, as well as on textiles worn during the summer months. Fishing Net (literally, just "net") is one of the easiest patterns to stitch and requires few knots. See the Doorway Curtain for a stitched example of this pattern.

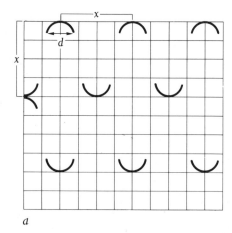

a

To draw: First calculate the diameter and placement of the semicircles. To do this, multiply the distance between semicircles (*x*) by $\frac{3}{8}$ to get the diameter of the circle template.

Examples:

x	$\times \frac{3}{8} =$	diameter (*d*)
$1''$		$\frac{3}{8}''$
$\frac{3}{4}''$		$\frac{9}{32}''$ (approx. $\frac{1}{4}''$)
$\frac{1}{2}''$		$\frac{3}{16}''$

Using the template, draw the semicircles on graph paper (Fig. *a*). Connect the semicircles with straight lines (dotted lines in Fig. *b*).

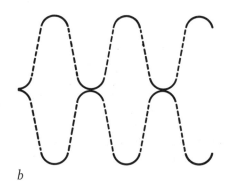

b

To stitch: Stitch each row of wavy lines in turn (Fig. *c*).

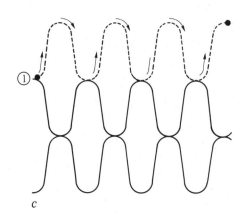

c

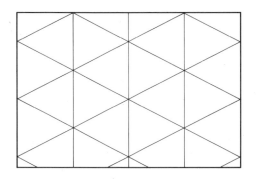

Fish Scales (*uroko*)

This arrangement of triangles was used to decorate prehistoric ceramic pieces in Japan. Fish Scales is one of the easiest patterns to draw and stitch. See the Doorway Curtain for a stitched example of the pattern.

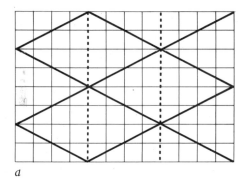

a

To draw: First draw a grid of diamonds on graph paper (solid lines in Fig. *a*). Then draw in straight, vertical lines that divide the diamonds in half (dotted lines).

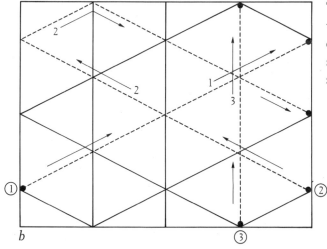

b

To stitch (Fig. *b*): Stitch each diagonal line in turn (1). To reduce the number of knots, turn the corner at the end of each line and continue stitching until you run out of thread (2). Finally, stitch the vertical lines (3).

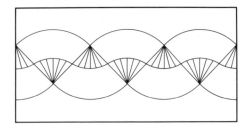

Folding Fans 1 (*senmen tsunagi*)

Folding fans are used in Japan for other reasons besides keeping a person cool on a hot summer day. In earlier times fans were part of court and religious formal attire. Folding fans are also used in Japanese dances and traditional dramas. In storytelling, a fan assumes a variety of roles such as a dagger, a butterfly, or a saw. The fan shape is a popular decorative motif on textiles, woodwork, paper, ceramics, and other media.

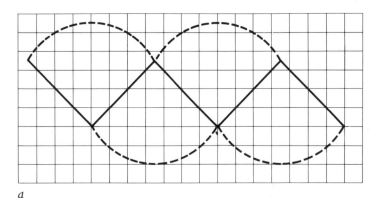

a

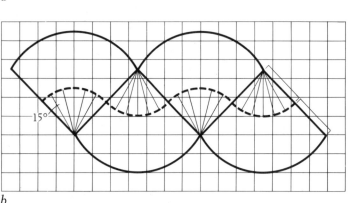

b

To draw: Before beginning, calculate the length of the fan and the circle template diameter. Use the following ratio:

$$\frac{3}{5} = \frac{\text{fan length}}{\text{template diameter}}$$

Examples:

fan length	diameter
$\frac{3}{4}''$	$1\frac{1}{4}''$
$1\frac{1}{4}''$	$2''$
$1\frac{1}{2}''$	$2\frac{1}{4}''$

Draw zigzag lines that meet at 90° angles (solid lines in Fig. *a*). Then draw curved lines using the circle template (dotted lines). The curves will *not* be semicircles. Mark the midpoint of each straight segment. Using the same size circle template, draw curved lines (dotted lines in Fig. *b*) using the marks as guides. Finally, draw "spokes," each of 15°, that radiate from the apex of the 90° angle. The spokes should end at the inner curved line.

To stitch: In order, stitch the zigzag lines, then the outer curved lines, then the inner curved lines (Fig. *c*), and finally the "spokes" (Fig. *d*).

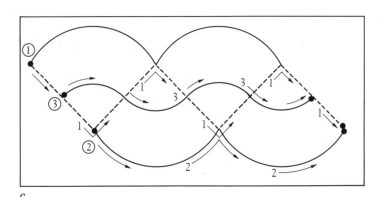

c

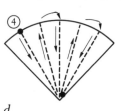

d

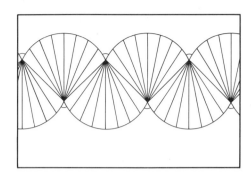

Folding Fans 2 (*senmen tsunagi*)

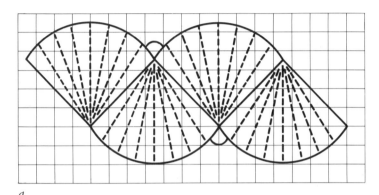

a

To draw (Fig. *a*): Before beginning, calculate the length of the fans and the circle template diameter. Use the same ratio as for Folding Fans 1. Draw zigzag lines that meet at 90° angles. Draw arcs connecting the corners using the circle template. The curves will *not* be semicircles. Draw "spokes" that divide each fan into eight equal sections (11¼° per section). Finally, draw a small, curved line opposite each 90° angle.

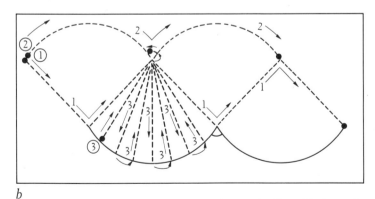

b

To stitch (Fig. *b*): In order, stitch the zigzag lines (1), the large curved lines (2), and then each set of spokes (3). After the final spoke in each set has been stitched, stitch the small curve.

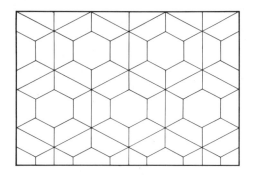

Hailstone (*arare kikko*)

This modern pattern requires many knots and is one of the more complicated to draw and stitch. Hailstone, a variation on the tortoise shell motif, is a winter pattern.

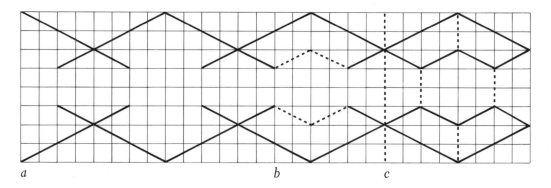

a   *b*   *c*

To draw: Draw long diagonal lines (Fig. *a*), then short diagonal lines (dotted lines in Fig. *b*), and finally all vertical lines (dotted lines in Fig. *c*).

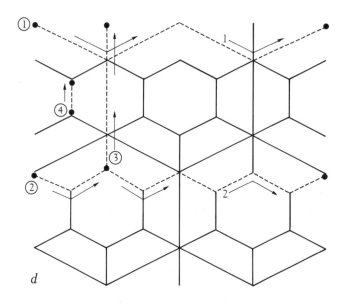

d

To stitch (Fig. *d*): In order, stitch large zigzag lines (1), then small zigzag lines (2), then long vertical segments (3), and finally short vertical segments (4).

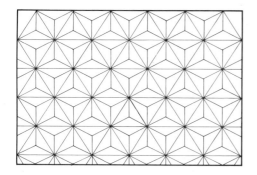

Hemp Leaf (*asa no ha*)

Hemp is a hardy plant that survives the cold of northern Japan and provides fiber from which linen is made. Hemp Leaf is an auspicious pattern that is often used to decorate babies' kimono in hopes that the infants will develop the vigor and strength of the hemp plant. This pattern is one of the most time-consuming to draw and stitch. It requires many knots and so is best for projects that will be lined.

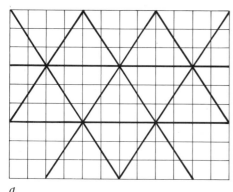

a

To draw: Draw a grid of either isosceles or equilateral triangles (2 or 3 equal sides). Isosceles triangles are shown here (Fig. *a*). Next draw parallel diagonal line segments (Fig. *b*). Finally, add the vertical segments (Fig. *c*).

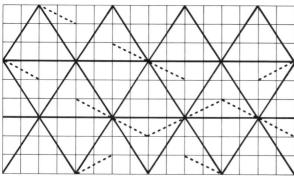

b

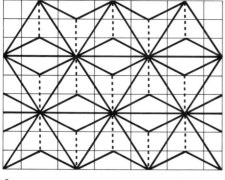

c

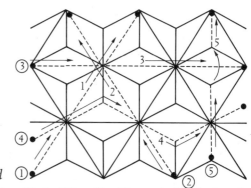

d

To stitch (Fig. *d*): First stitch all the diagonal lines (1, 2). Then, in order, stitch the horizontal lines (3), the zigzag lines (4), and the vertical segments (5).

45

Hydrangea (*ajisai*)

The hydrangea is a popular garden flower in Japan. It blooms during the rainy season and suggests summer when used as a decorative motif. Stitch this design using the counted-thread method. Draw the design on paper first even though the pattern will not be transferred to the fabric; the drawing will serve as a guide for stitching.

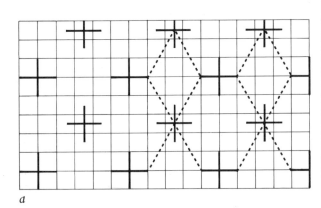

a

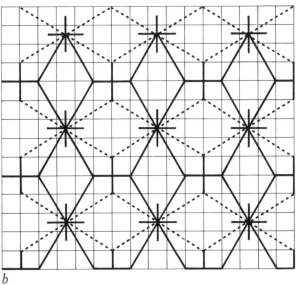

b

To draw: Draw evenly spaced plus signs (Fig. *a*). The lines should be equal in length. Connect the centers of the plus signs in every other vertical column to the tips of neighboring plus signs (dotted lines in Fig. *a*). Finally, connect the centers of the remaining plus signs to the tips of their neighboring plus signs to complete the design (Fig. *b*).

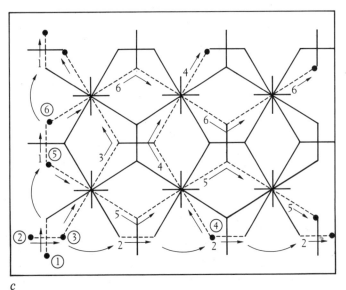

c

To stitch (Fig. *c*): Use the counted-thread technique to stitch this design. First stitch the vertical lines (1). Note that the lines and spaces are not equal in length. For example, the lines may be four threads long and the spaces six threads long. Stitch the horizontal lines to form the plus signs (2). Do not stitch the diagonal lines by passing the needle through the fabric. Instead, weave the sewing thread under the tips of the plus signs, passing the thread under the centers of intervening plus marks as you go (3–6). Try to keep the tension even while weaving—don't pull the thread too tight or let it get too slack.

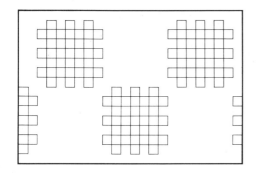

Latticed Ikat (*koshi-gasuri*)

Ikat is a dyeing technique used to decorate textiles. Skeins of thread are tie-dyed with patterns before they are woven. The patterns emerge as the threads are woven into cloth. Japanese ikat (*kasuri*) typically consists of white patterning on an indigo background. Cotton ikat fabrics are still popular for summer kimonos, work jackets, and trousers, especially in the countryside.

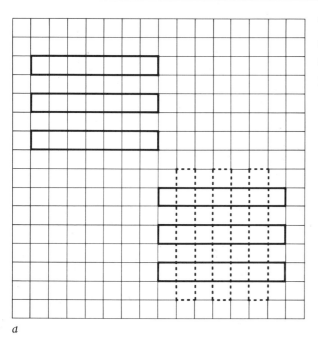

a

To draw (Fig. *a*): Draw three rectangles that are each one block wide and seven blocks long. Then draw three more rectangles of the same size perpendicular to the original rectangles (dotted lines).

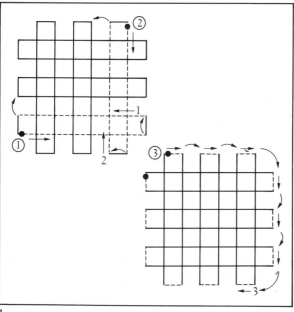

b

To stitch (Fig. *b*): Stitch the horizontal lines, passing the thread behind the fabric at the end of each row, before starting the next row (1). Stitch the vertical rows in the same manner (2). Stitch the short ends of each rectangle in the lattice pattern (3).

Linked Diamonds (*kumibishi*)

This pattern requires many knots and is one of the more complicated to draw and stitch.

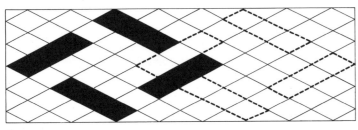

a

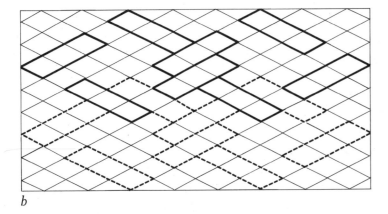

b

To draw: Use triangular grid graph paper to draw this design. Begin by drawing a diamond (shaded in illustration) composed of four parallelograms (solid lines in Fig. *a*). Draw another diamond that links horizontally with the first diamond (dotted lines). Continue by adding diamonds that link vertically to complete the repeating design (Fig. *b*).

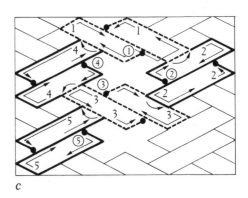

c

To stitch (Fig. *c*): Stitch the first pair of adjacent parallelograms (1). Stitch subsequent pairs of parallelograms (2–5), passing the thread to the back of the fabric where necessary.

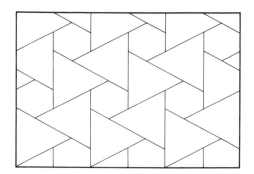

Linked Hexagons (*musubi kikko*)

This pattern is easy to draw and stitch but results in many loops of thread behind the fabric when completed. Use this pattern for lined projects.

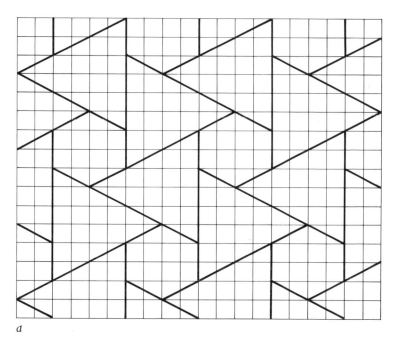

a

To draw: Use the grid to draw connecting triangles and hexagons (Fig. *a*). In this example, each triangle has a base of six blocks and a height of six blocks.

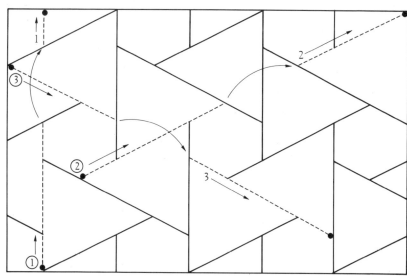

b

To stitch (Fig. *b*): Stitch the vertical lines (1). Then stitch the diagonal lines (2, 3).

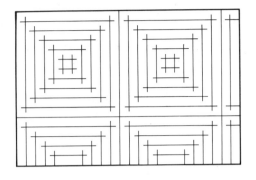

Measuring Boxes (*masu sashi*)

This pattern represents boxes of different sizes nestled inside one another. Large, square wooden boxes were used in old Japan to measure rice. The smaller boxes are still used as cups for drinking Japanese saké. Textiles decorated with patterns of larger boxes were worn by the elders, while younger folk would wear patterns of smaller boxes. In this way, a person's general age could be inferred from the size of the pattern on his or her kimono.

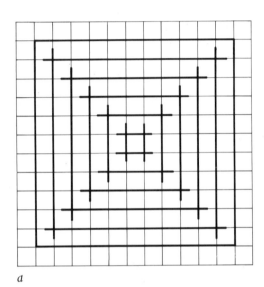

a

To draw (Fig. *a*): Use graph paper to draw each set of concentric squares. Extend the lines a little at each corner. Begin by drawing the center box and continue by drawing each box in order of increasing size. Draw a large square around each set of measuring boxes.

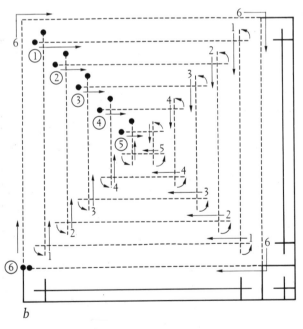

b

To stitch (Fig. *b*): Within a large square, stitch each side of the largest measuring box (1). At the corners, pass the thread to the back of the fabric and begin stitching the nearest perpendicular side. In the same manner, stitch each measuring box in order of decreasing size (2–5). Finally, stitch the horizontal and vertical lines to establish large squares around each set of nested boxes (6).

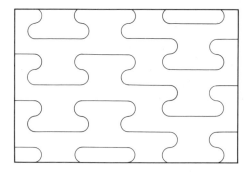

Mist (*kasumi tsunagi*)

Clouds and mist became popular motifs around the mid-seventh century. During the following centuries, gold and silver dust was employed to depict these motifs on scrolls. Clouds and mist appeared in paintings of daily court life, too; they concealed parts of the scene from view while adding motion, emotion, and space to the composition. This stylized pattern of swirling misty clouds is easy to draw and stitch.

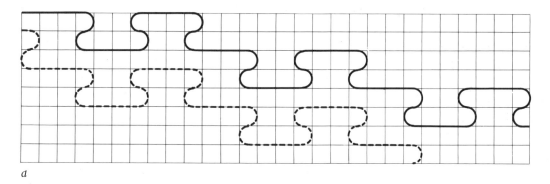

a

To draw (Fig. *a*): Before beginning, calculate the length of each section. Each section includes two semicircles and the connecting line between them. The section length is four times the diameter of the circle template used to draw the semicircles.

Examples:

diameter	× 4 =	section length
¼″		1″
½″		2″
¾″		3″

Using the grid as a guide, draw the semicircles and connecting lines to form a wavy line. Draw the next row of connecting semicircles and lines, continuing until the area to be decorated is filled.

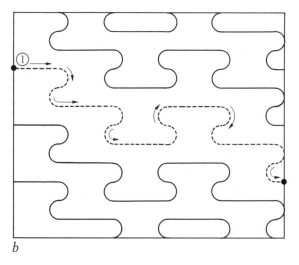

b

To stitch (Fig. *b*): Stitch each undulating line in turn.

51

Mountains 1 (*yama sashi*)

Mountains can be seen everywhere in Japan since they comprise about 80% of the country's land area. This is one of the oldest sashiko patterns, used when designs were limited to vertical and horizontal lines. It is one of the easiest to draw and stitch.

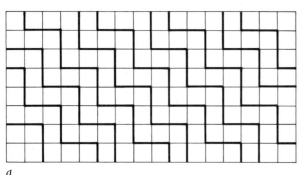

a

To draw (Fig. *a*): Count the blocks as you draw parallel rows of zigzag lines.

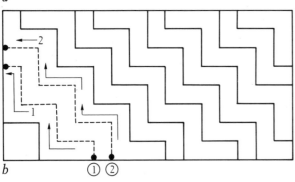

b ① ②

To stitch (Fig. *b*): Stitch each row of zigzag lines in turn.

Mountains 2 (*yama sashi*)

For this version of the Mountains pattern, use longer vertical and horizontal lines.

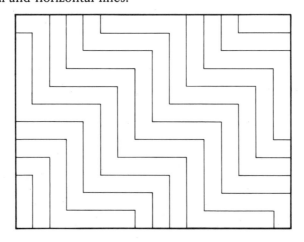

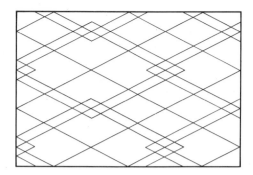

Overlapping Diamonds (*narihira waribishi*)

This pattern is moderately complicated to draw yet easy to stitch.

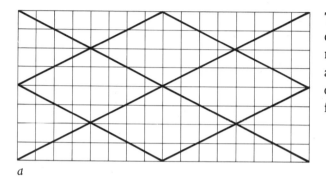

a

To draw: Draw diagonal lines to form a grid of diamonds (Fig. *a*). Note that four small diamonds make one large diamond. Draw parallel lines around sets of four small diamonds. Not every set of four diamonds will be enclosed. Follow Figure *b* for the correct placement of the parallel lines.

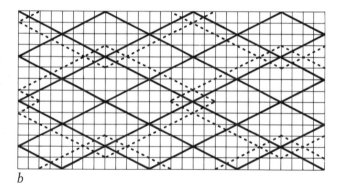

b

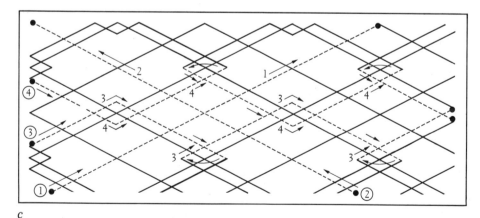

c

To stitch (Fig. *c*): Stitch the long diagonal lines (1, 2). Stitch the zigzag lines (3, 4). Pass the thread behind the fabric at the curved arrows.

53

Pampas Grass (nowaki)

Pampas grass, one of the symbols of autumn, is a popular motif in textile decoration. This classic stylized motif depicts pampas grass bending in the wind. The pattern is one of the simplest to draw and stitch. See the Wrapping Cloth project for a stitched example of this pattern.

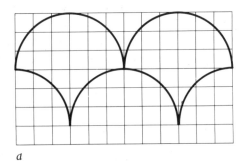

a

To draw: Use a circle template to draw large semicircles (Fig. *a*). Use the same size template to draw the shorter blades of grass (Fig. *b*).

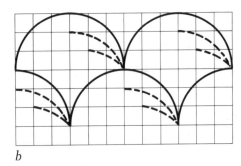

b

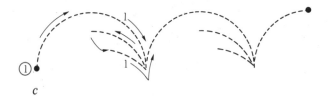

c

To stitch (Fig. *c*): Stitch each semicircle and the grass within it before proceeding to the next semicircle. Stitch in the order shown.

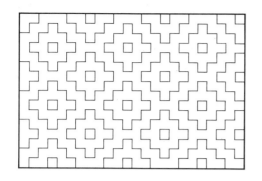

Persimmon Flower (*kaki no hana*)

This is one of the original patterns of early sashiko stitching. If using the counted-thread stitching technique, there is no need to draw the pattern. See the Knickknack Bag project for a stitched example of the pattern.

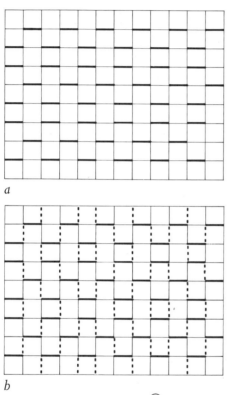

a

b

To draw: Following the grid, draw rows of horizontal dashes, each dash corresponding to one side of a grid box (Fig. *a*). Note that every third row is staggered. Next draw vertical dashed lines (dotted lines in Fig. *b*). Alternatively, draw each "blossom" and its square center in turn.

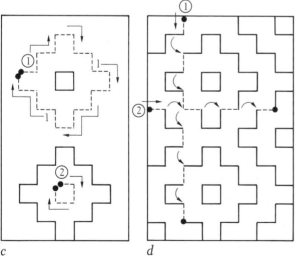

c

d

To stitch:

REGULAR METHOD (Fig. *c*): Stitch a blossom (1) and its center (2) before proceeding to the next blossom. This method is best for large-scale designs.

COUNTED-THREAD METHOD (Fig. *d*): This, the original method used, is appropriate when stitching on evenweave fabric. There is no need to transfer the design onto the fabric. Instead, counting threads as you go, stitch all the warp threads and then all the weft threads. For example, stitch over 5 warp (or weft) threads and under 5, over 5 and under 5, etc. Stitch all vertical rows (1) before stitching horizontal rows (2).

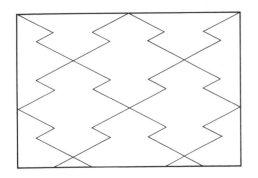

Pine Bark (*matsukawa bishi*)

This pattern is derived from the crackled bark of the pine tree. A hardy tree that survives the cold winters, pine is a symbol of perseverance and good fortune. This sashiko pattern is one of the easiest to stitch. You may wish to use a single lozenge shape (or several grouped together) as an outline to be filled in with other sashiko patterns. See the Doorway Curtain for a stitched example of the pattern.

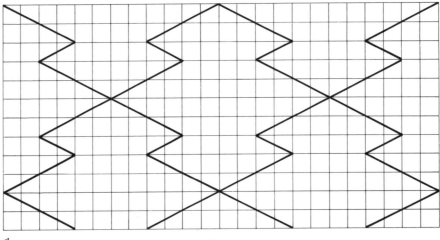

a

To draw (Fig. *a*): Simply count the blocks (for example, starting at the top left corner, 4 right and 2 down, 2 left and 1 down, etc.) as you draw the zigzag lines.

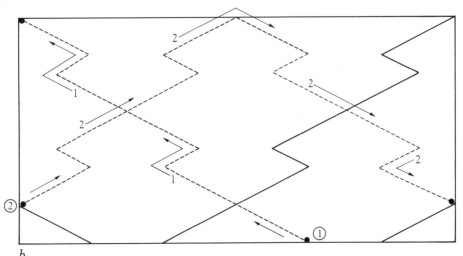

b

To stitch (Fig. *b*): Stitch each zigzag line in turn (1). Or, to reduce the number of knots, turn a corner at the end of the zigzag line and continue to stitch connecting zigzag lines (2).

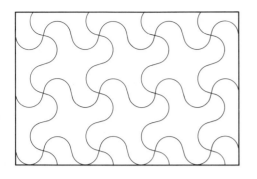

Plovers (*chidori tsunagi*)

Chidori, the Japanese word for plover, literally means "one thousand birds." This is because plovers fly in large numbers when they visit Japanese shores in autumn. This stylized pattern of connecting semicircles represents the outlines of plovers in flight. Plovers is one of the simplest patterns to draw and stitch. See the Wrapping Cloth for a stitched example of the pattern.

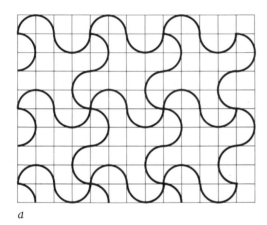

a

To draw (Fig. *a*): Draw semicircles with a compass or circle template, using the grid as a guide. Count the blocks to ensure proper placement of each row of horizontal and vertical wavy lines.

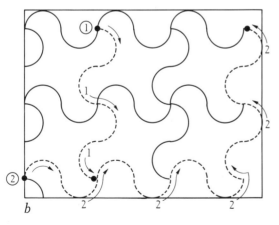

b

To stitch (Fig. *b*): Stitch vertical wavy lines (1) and then stitch horizontal wavy lines. To reduce the number of knots, turn the corner at the end of a wavy line and continue along a perpendicular line of stitching (2).

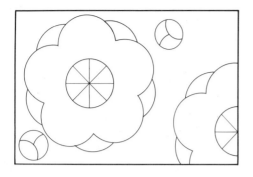

Plum Blossom (*ume no hana*)

Plum blossoms bloom in early spring when the air is still very cold, so they symbolize courage. The blossoms appear before the leaves—delicate pink and white against dark branches. As a decorative motif, plum blossoms and the nightingale often appear together as symbols of the coming spring.

a

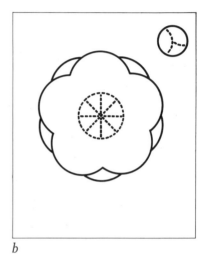

b

To draw: Make a template of cardboard or plastic in the shape of a five-petalled flower. Trace the template, then rotate the template and draw more petals between the first petals (Fig. *a*). Draw in the center of the blossom using a circular template (Fig. *b*). Then add evenly spaced "spokes." With a small circle template, draw in randomly placed buds. To each bud add two curved lines to represent the folded petals.

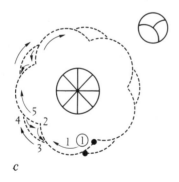

c

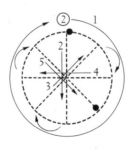

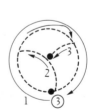

To stitch (Fig. *c*): Stitch the petals of each blossom (1). Pass the thread behind the fabric when starting and ending the overlapping petals. Next stitch the center of each blossom (2): first stitch the circle and then the spokes. Pass the thread behind the fabric when beginning and ending a spoke. Stitch each bud (3): first stitch the circle and then the lines inside the circle.

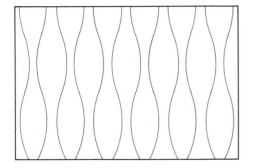

Rising Steam (*tatewaku*)

Members of the Japanese court in the ninth to twelfth centuries wore ceremonial garments decorated with Rising Steam in combination with clouds, honeysuckle, and other motifs arranged between the undulating lines. This pattern is not one of the easiest to draw, but it is very easy to stitch and requires few knots. See the Doorway Curtain for a stitched example of this pattern.

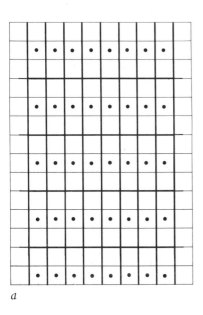

a

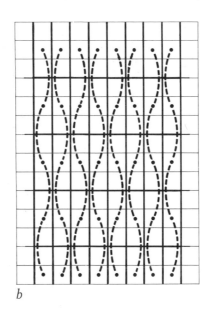

b

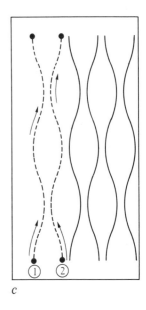

c

To draw: Use a circle template with a grid of rectangles. Calculate the circle template size using the following ratio:

1	:	3	:	7
(rectangle width)		(rectangle length)		(circle diameter)

Examples:

Rectangle Width	Rectangle Length	Circle Diameter
¼"	¾"	1¾"
½"	1½"	3½"

Lightly draw a grid of rectangles, each of which is three times as long as it is wide (Fig. *a*). (This grid is just a guide and not part of the finished pattern.) Draw a dot at the center of each rectangle. Connect the dots using the circle template as a guide. Alternate the direction of the arc to form undulating lines (Fig. *b*).

To stitch (Fig. *c*): Stitch each undulating line in turn.

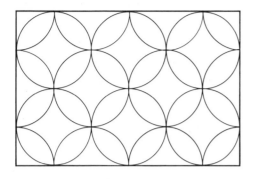

Seven Treasures 1 (*shippo tsunagi*)

This design is common to many cultures. In the United States, quilters know it by such names as the Double Wedding Ring and Cathedral Window. In Japan, the motif was often used to decorate Buddhist art. The pattern is said to represent the seven precious jewels mentioned in Buddhist sutras: agate, amber, coral, gold, lapis lazuli, pearl, and silver. See the Triangle Bag for a stitched example of this pattern.

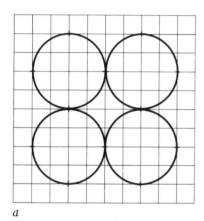

a

To draw: Draw rows of touching circles using a circle template. Mark the quarter points of each circle (Fig. *a*). Draw overlapping circles using the quarter-point marks as guides for even placement (Fig. *b*).

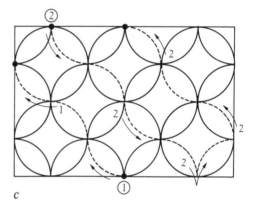

c

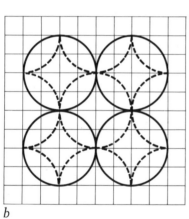

b

To stitch (Fig. *c*): There is no set order for stitching the Seven Treasures pattern. The only rule is: Stitch long wavy lines, not individual circles (1). The design will slowly emerge as you stitch the wavy lines. To reduce the number of knots necessary, turn the corner at the end of a wavy line and continue stitching in the opposite direction until you run out of thread (2).

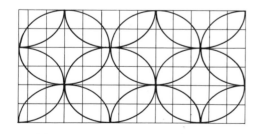

Seven Treasures 2 (*shippo tsunagi*)

Use an oval template instead of a circular one to draw this modified version of the basic Seven Treasures design.

Seven Treasures 3 (*maru shippo*)

This pattern requires many knots and is one of the more complicated to draw and stitch. See the Doorway Curtain for a stitched example of this pattern.

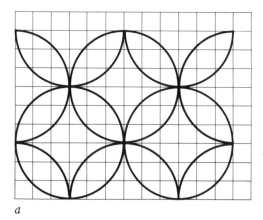

a

To draw: Calculate the diameters of the three circle templates before beginning. The ratio of the diameters is 3 : 10 : 12. Some examples:

Small	Medium	Large
1/4"	7/8"	1"
3/8"	1 1/4"	1 1/2"
1/2"	1 2/3"	2"
3/4"	2 1/2"	3"

Using the large circle template, draw the Seven Treasures 1 pattern (Fig. *a*). With the small template, draw circles at the quarter points of the large circles (Fig. *b*). With the medium-size template, draw circles centered within the large circles. Erase all lines that fall within the small circles.

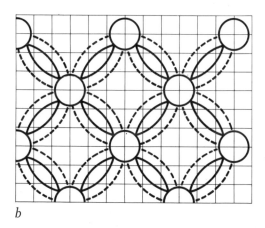

b

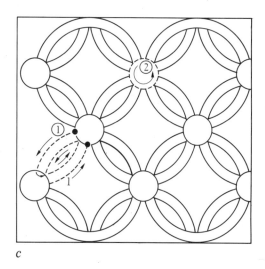

c

To stitch (Fig. *c*): First stitch each set of curved lines connecting the small circles (1). Then stitch the small circles (2).

61

Silk Weave 1 (sayagata)

This pattern was introduced to Japan on Ming-period Chinese textiles. In Japan, the design traditionally appeared on a figured silk weave called *saya*, so it is called the *saya* pattern. In English, the pattern is also known as Monk's Maze. Despite its complicated appearance, this design is one of the simplest to stitch and requires only a few knots. For a stitched example, see the Wrapping Cloth project.

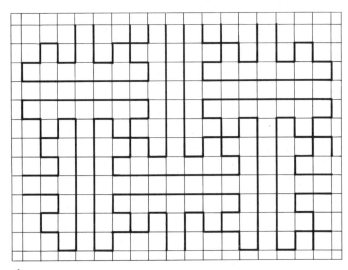

a

To draw (Fig. *a*): Draw this design by counting blocks as you follow the stitch order numbers in Figure *b*.

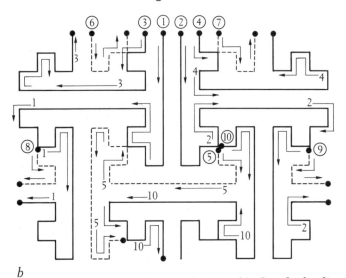

b

To stitch (Fig. *b*): Stitch the lines of the pattern in the same manner they were drawn, following the numbered order shown (1–10).

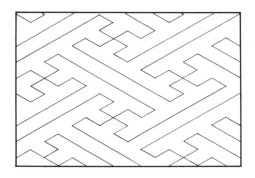

Silk Weave 2 (*sayagata*)

For this variation on the *saya* pattern, use a triangular grid (Fig. *a*) and follow the same drawing and stitching instructions as for Silk Weave 1. For a stitched example of the pattern, see the Floor Cushion project.

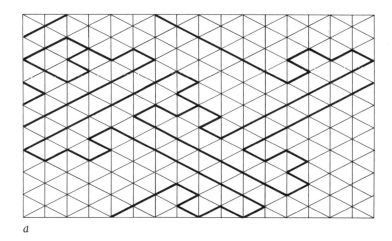

a

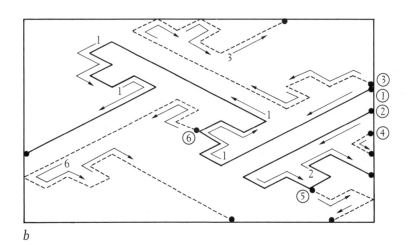

b

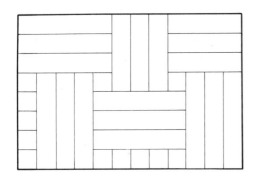

Stone Pavement (ishi-datami)

This design represents cut rock arranged to form a patterned walkway (ishi-datami). A path of this kind may be found near the entrance to a house or within a garden. Another name for this geometric design is sankuzushi— divining blocks laid out in random order. In Japan, fortunes are read by placing narrow blocks side by side. This pattern is easy to draw but requires many knots when stitching.

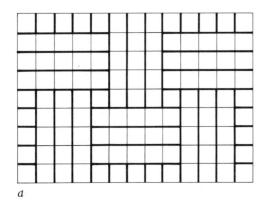

a

To draw (Fig. a): Use graph paper to draw sets of four parallel lines. Each line is 5 blocks long.

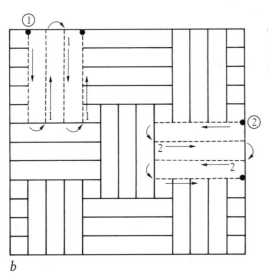

b

To stitch (Fig. b): Stitch each group of four lines in a continuous manner by passing the thread behind the fabric to start the next line.

Sun Symbol (*hiragumi manji tsunagi*)

This pattern is composed of interlocking swastika-like shapes called *manji*. An ancient propitious symbol of Indo-Aryan origin, the *manji* represents the sun and the cosmos. The shape is sometimes called "four-legged chicken" after its resemblance to a chicken running at full tilt. Sun Symbol is a simple pattern to draw and stitch, but since it requires quite a few knots, it is best for projects that will be lined.

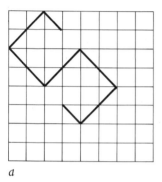

a

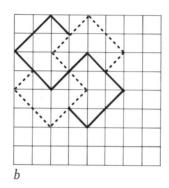

b

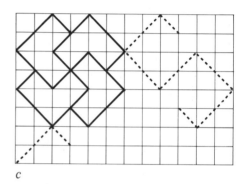

c

To draw: Count the blocks and draw an **S** shape (Fig. *a*). Count the blocks and draw another **S** shape, positioning it to link with the first (dotted lines in Fig. *b*). Continue drawing connecting **S** shapes (Fig. *c*).

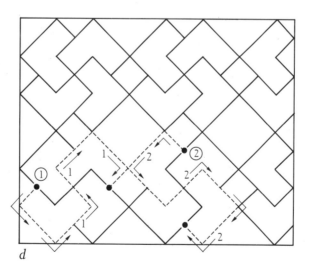

d

To stitch (Fig. *d*): Stitch all the **S** shapes that lean in one direction (1). Then stitch all the **S** shapes that lean in the other direction (2).

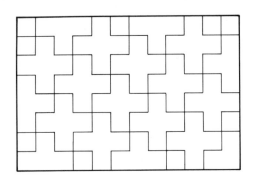

"Ten" Pattern (*juji tsunagi*)

This design depicts the Japanese (and Chinese) ideogram for the number ten (+). The pattern requires few knots and is easy to draw and stitch.

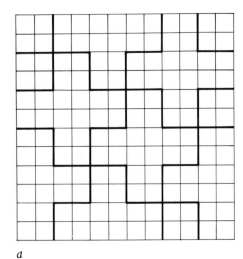

a

To draw (Fig. *a*): Draw rows of vertical and horizontal "stairs," counting the graph-paper blocks as you go (e.g., 2 blocks right, 4 blocks up, 2 blocks right, 4 blocks up, etc.).

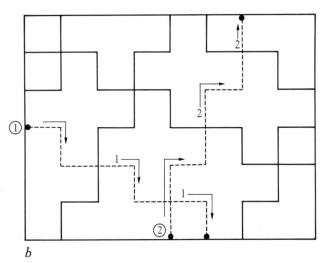

b

To stitch (Fig. *b*): Stitch rows that progress horizontally (1) and then rows that progress vertically (2).

Tortoise Shell 1 (*kikko*)

The tortoise has been a symbol of longevity since ancient times. According to Chinese legend, a tortoise supported the heavens and the sacred tortoise lives for ten thousand years. The auspicious Tortoise Shell pattern was most popular in Japan during the ninth through twelfth centuries. This design is somewhat complicated to draw and stitch and requires many knots.

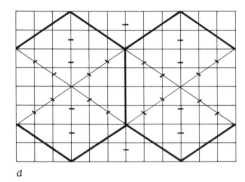

a

To draw: Draw a grid of isosceles triangles (2 equal sides) on graph paper (Fig. *a*). In this example, the triangles have a base of 4 blocks and a height of 3 blocks. Some of the lines are guidelines and will not be part of the finished design, so draw lightly. Darken the lines that form hexagons (Fig. *b*). Then mark the points that divide each radiating spoke into three equal parts. Connect the points to form two concentric hexagons within each large hexagon (Fig. *b*).

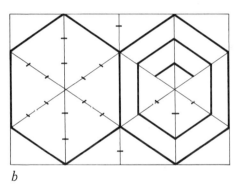

b

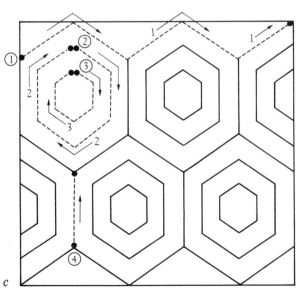

c

To stitch (Fig. *c*): In order, stitch zigzag lines (1), then concentric hexagons (2, 3), and finally vertical lines (4).

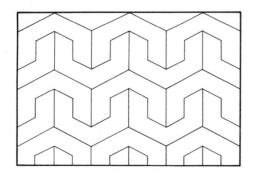

Tortoise Shell 2 (*mukai kikko*)

This design is relatively easy to draw but requires many knots.

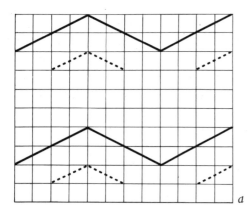

a

To draw: Draw large parallel zigzag lines (solid lines in Fig. *a*). Draw inverted Vs (dotted lines). Draw vertical segments (dotted lines in Fig. *b*). Draw Vs (dotted lines in Fig. *c*).

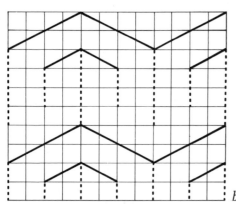

b

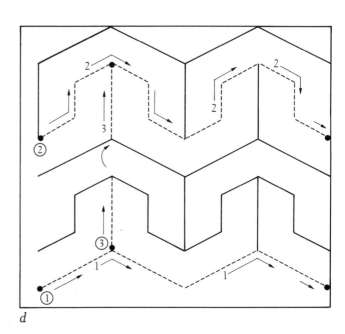

d

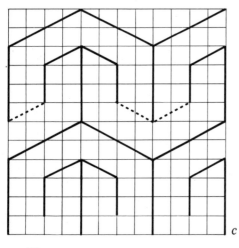

c

To stitch (Fig. *d*): In order, stitch large zigzag lines (1), then rows of notched lines (2), and finally vertical segments (3).

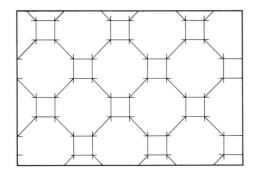

Water Wells (*igeta ni hakkaku tsunagi*)

Wells in Japanese villages were a place where people gathered to socialize and exchange gossip. The Water Wells pattern consists of the square rims of water wells connected to form octagons. The design is easy to draw and stitch, but it results in many loops of thread on the back of the fabric when completed. Use for lined projects.

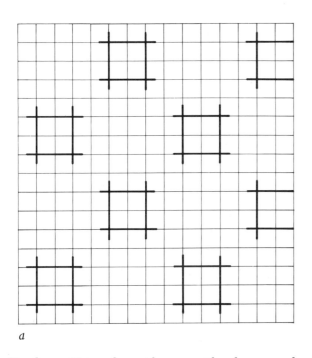

a

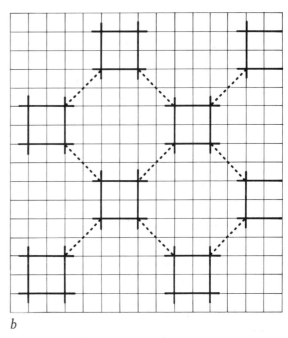

b

To draw: Using the grid as a guide, draw evenly spaced squares (Fig. *a*). Extend the lines a little at the corners (extended a half block in this example).

Connect the corners of the squares with diagonal lines (Fig. *b*).

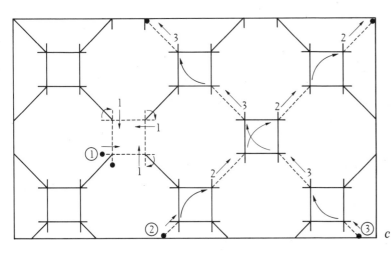

c

To stitch (Fig. *c*): Stitch each square separately (1). Stitch the diagonal lines (2, 3). Pass the thread behind the fabric at the squares.

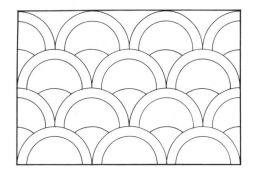

Waves 1 (*seigaiha*)

Seigaiha, the Japanese name of this design, literally means "blue ocean waves." This is the name given to one of the dances performed by Prince Genji of the classic novel *Tale of Genji.* Waves is one of the easiest designs to draw and stitch. See the Doorway Curtain for a stitched example of the pattern.

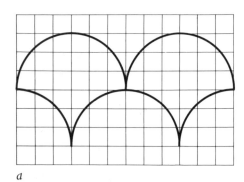

a

To draw: Two circle templates are needed to draw this design. The larger circle is used to draw the outer arc of each wave, while the smaller circle is used to draw the two inner arcs. Calculate the diameters of the circles as follows: Diameter of large circle × ¾ = diameter of small circle.

Examples:

Large circle diameter	Small circle diameter
1″	¾″
1½″	1⅛″
3″	2¼″

Draw rows of semicircles using the large circle template (Fig. *a*). Draw the inner arcs using the small circle template (Fig. *b*).

b

To stitch:

METHOD 1 (Fig. *c*): Stitch each row of large semicircles (1). Stitch each row of medium-size arcs, passing the thread behind the fabric between arcs (2). Finally, stitch each row of small arcs (3).

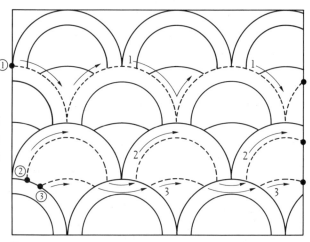

c

METHOD 2 (Fig. *d*): Use this method if the gaps between the small or medium-size arcs are large (1″ or more). Stitch each set of three arcs before starting the next set (1).

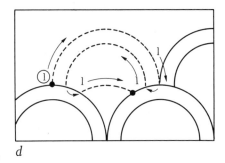

d

Waves 2 (*seigaiha*)

For this variation on the basic Waves pattern, use oval templates instead of circular templates.

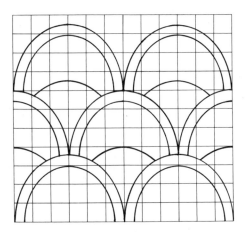

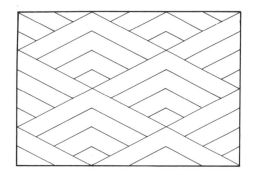

Waves 3 (*hishi seigaiha*)

This diamond-shaped variation on one of the most popular motifs in Japan is used to decorate textiles, ceramics, wood, metal, and lacquerware. The pattern is easy to draw and stitch. See the Wrapping Cloth for a stitched example of the design.

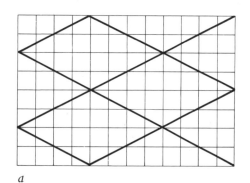

a

To draw: Draw a grid of diamonds on graph paper (Fig. *a*). Draw parallel straight lines in one half of each diamond (Fig. *b*). Draw the mirror image of these lines in the other half of each diamond (dotted lines in Fig. *c*).

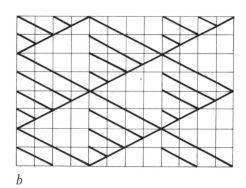

b

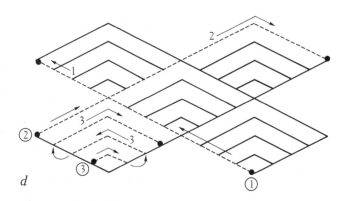

c

d

To stitch (Fig. *d*): Stitch long diagonal lines (1). To reduce the number of knots, turn the corner and continue on to connecting diagonal lines (2). Stitch each set of inner "waves" with one length of thread (3).

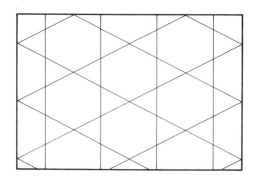

Woven Bamboo (*kagome*)

This pattern represents strips of bamboo that are woven together in an open weave. Since the weave is very open, it is a popular choice for the shades of bamboo-and-paper lanterns in summer. Woven Bamboo is one of the easiest patterns to draw and stitch.

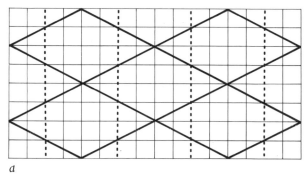

a

To draw (Fig. *a*): Draw a grid of diamonds. Then draw in evenly spaced vertical lines.

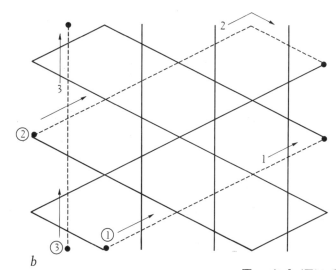

b

To stitch (Fig. *b*): Stitch each diagonal line (1). To reduce the number of knots, turn the corner and continue stitching down a connecting diagonal line (2). Stitch the vertical lines (3).

Part
THREE

Projects

Presented in this chapter are instructions for constructing and positioning sashiko patterns on five traditional Japanese items that have proved popular with American sewers: a knickknack bag, an ingeniously designed carrying bag, floor cushions, a doorway curtain, and a square cloth for wrapping and carrying things. All are practical and well suited to Western lifestyles.

With minor alterations, the project patterns can be used to make common Western items as well. The wrapping cloth may serve as an elegant shawl or, enlarged, as a table cloth or, reduced in size, as a scarf, handkerchief, or coaster. Similarly, the floor cushions made smaller become sofa throw pillows. If left a flat rectangle, the triangle purse pattern may be used to make a table runner, and the doorway curtain may be easily adapted for use as a window curtain.

The ultimate sashiko project, covered amply in other books, may well be the Western quilt itself. Sashiko makes an excellent background stitch for securing the layers of fabric and batting together. A sashiko-stitched quilt also bridges the sewing traditions of the two cultures nicely. Both sashiko quilting and Western quilting are functional needle arts with humble origins. Both evolved in a spirit of respect for materials. And both embody the warmth of the community in which they were created.

The yardage requirements listed for each project allow for ⅛ yard (4½″) of shrinkage. Prewash and iron all fabrics before cutting into them. Narrow Japanese fabrics (about 15″ wide) are usually not preshrunk in Japan, but taking this precaution will prevent unpleasant surprises later on. For Japanese cotton fabrics, handwashing is recommended.

Although some Japanese sewing techniques are used in the assembly of the projects, feel free to substitute Western methods. There is no need to stitch all the seams by hand while sitting on the floor—a sewing machine and chair will yield just as beautiful results. Nevertheless, two traditional techniques are worth a try: pattern mapping and the overlap fold.

The construction of each project begins with the Japanese pattern-mapping technique (*saidanzu*). Because kimonos, jackets, and trousers are made entirely of rectangular fabric pieces, paper patterns have been unnecessary throughout the history of Japanese sewing.

Instead of paper patterns, the Japanese use a "pattern map"—a drawing of the laid-out rectangles with dimensions written in. The drawing is often accompanied by a chart that

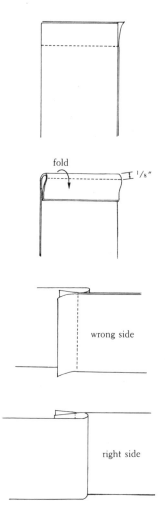

fold

$^1/_8''$

wrong side

right side

Making a *kise* fold

provides dimensions for making various sizes of a garment. When cutting the pieces needed to construct a garment, the length and width measurements of the rectangles are marked directly on the fabric and warp or weft threads are pulled out of the marked points. The pulled threads become the cutting lines. (The grain of most fabrics, however, is not straight; in this case, mark the material with a ruler and tailor's chalk and then cut.)

Seams of Japanese garments are hidden from view on the right side of the fabric by a tiny fold of fabric. The addition of this overlap on seams is a technique used extensively in sewing projects of all kinds. This small overlap is called a *kise*.

To make a *kise* fold, sew a seam and press it lightly on the wrong side. Then fold the seam allowance of both layers over so that there is a ⅛″ fold above the stitches. Press this fold.

When constructing a seam, be careful to keep the *kise* fold intact. Do not open and press the seam allowances as in Western sewing.

When instructions say to make a *kise* (overlap fold) toward the lining, it means that the lining fabric should be on top, facing up, before the seam allowance is folded over and pressed. The triangle bag and floor cushions call for *kise* folds.

Some of the stitches used in various projects are described below: The **tacking** or **basting stitch** is used in the knickknack bag and the floor cushion. The **blindstitched hem** is used in the doorway curtain. The **triplefold blindstitched hem** is used in the doorway curtain and the wrapping cloth. The **"plover"** (*chidori-kagari*) or **herringbone stitch** is used to join the panels in the doorway curtain.

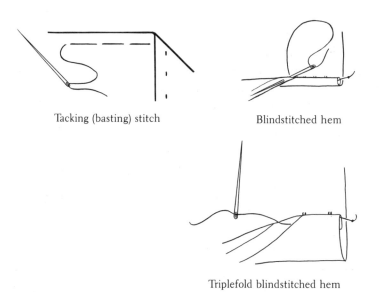

Tacking (basting) stitch

Blindstitched hem

Triplefold blindstitched hem

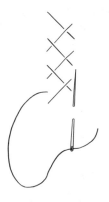

"Plover" stitch

Knickknack Bag (color photo on back cover)

In feudal Japan, the common people carried their money in small cloth bags with long purse strings. These bags were generally made of scraps of cloth, although merchants carried ones made of more durable leather. In addition, the Japanese carried amulet cases, tobacco pouches, and all sorts of cloth bags and pouches for holding small articles. These bags were made in the shapes of dolls, rectangles, tubes, and fans and were used to hold pipes, plectrums (picks for stringed instruments), combs, and utensils for the tea ceremony. The bags were small enough to tuck into the waist sash, or under the long collar at the bosom, or into the dangling sleeve of the traditional kimono.

The following project is a modern version of one kind of bag, called a *komono-ire*, designed to hold small objects. This adaptation is larger than its prototype and can be used as a clutch purse or to hold cosmetics, jewelry, handkerchiefs, or any small object.

MATERIALS
fabric: ⅝ yd* (10″ × 17″)
lining: ⅝ yd* (9½″ × 16½″)
polyester fleece, batting or interfacing: ⅝ yd* (9½″ × 16½″) (*optional*)
thread: pearl cotton #5 for sashiko and sewing thread to match fabric
*Note: Yardage allows for ⅛ yard shrinkage.

1. Cut out fabric and lining (Fig. *a*). A 27-count linen evenweave fabric was used here. *Optional*: For a padded bag, cut out batting; for extra body, cut out interfacing. Baste batting or interfacing to the wrong side of the lining (Fig. *b*).

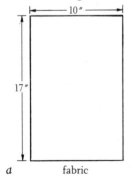

a   fabric

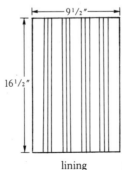

lining

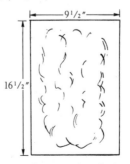

batting, fleece, or interfacing (optional)

b

2. Transfer sashiko design to the fabric and stitch (Fig. *c*). (If evenweave fabric is used, there is no need to transfer the design.) One strand of pearl cotton #5 and the Persimmon Flower pattern were used here; every three threads were stitched with the counted-thread method.

3. Pin lining to fabric, right sides together, and stitch the top and bottom seams, gathering the fabric slightly to fit the lining width (Fig. *d*). Trim seam allowance.

4. Turn right-side out. Adjust the lining so it extends $1/8''$ beyond the fabric. Baste seam to lining with a tacking stitch (Fig. *e*; see also p. 77). Press. Press top seam allowances toward the lining.

5. Turn so right sides are together. Fold and pin fabric and lining as shown in Figure *f*. Press.

6. Stitch $1/2''$ side seams, leaving a 2″ opening on one side (Fig. *g*).

7. Clip corners and turn bag right-side out through the 2″ opening.

8. Blindstitch the opening closed. Press.

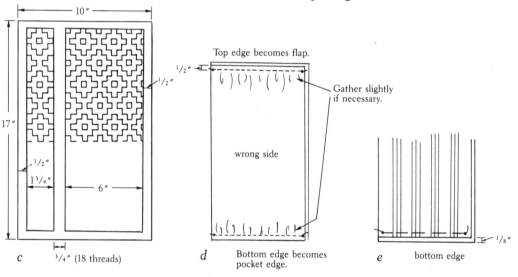

c $3/4''$ (18 threads)

d Top edge becomes flap.
Gather slightly if necessary.
wrong side
Bottom edge becomes pocket edge.

e bottom edge

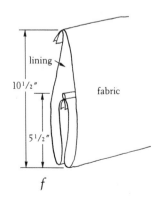

f lining fabric $10 1/2''$ $5 1/2''$

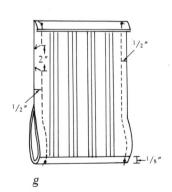

g

Triangle Bag (color photo on back cover)

The construction of the triangle bag (*sankaku-bukuro*) is yet another example of conservation and resourcefulness in the use of fabric—quite in keeping with the spirit of sashiko. A bag of any size can be made as long as you start out with a rectangle of fabric that is three times as long as it is wide.

Two simple folds and a few seams are all that is required to make this bag, which is perfect for toting books, a box lunch, knitting projects, or shopping purchases. The triangle bag works on the same principle as the Japanese wrapping cloth—items are inserted into the bag and the two ends that are tied in a square knot become the handle. The bag can be folded into a compact square until it is needed.

This ingenious design is so simple that children in Japan learn to make the bag in their first-grade classes.

MATERIALS
> fabric: 1⅜ yd* (15″ × 45″) or any rectangle with a length that
>   is three times the width measurement
> lining: same as fabric
> thread: white crochet thread for sashiko and sewing thread to
>   match fabric
> *Note: Yardage allows for ⅛ yard shrinkage.

1. Cut out fabric and lining (Fig. *a*).
2. Place lining right-side up on a flat surface. Fold over right third of rectangle and stitch bottom seam, right sides together (Fig. *b*). Add a *kise* fold (Fig. *c*; see also p. 77). Temporarily fold top layer down, so it's out of the way (Fig. *d*).
3. Fold over left third of lining rectangle and stitch top seam, right sides together, leaving a 3″ opening in the center of the seam (Fig. *e*). Make sure to stitch through only two layers. Add a *kise* fold (Fig. *f*).

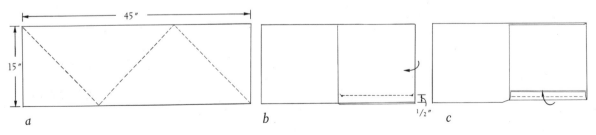

45″

15″

a   b   ½″   c

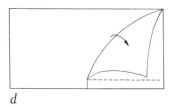

d

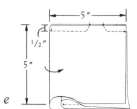

e

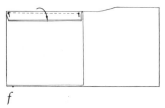

f

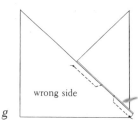

wrong side

g

4. Open lining and iron seams, taking care to keep *kise* folds intact (Fig. *g*). Turn lining right-side out.

5. Transfer the sashiko pattern to the fabric and stitch (Fig. *h*). Seven Treasures 1 is used in this example. Three other possible pattern arrangements are also shown.

6. Place fabric right-side up on a flat surface. Fold over right third of the rectangle toward the center of the fabric. Sew top seam, right sides together (Fig. *i*). Add a *kise* fold (Fig. *f*).

7. Fold top layer up, out of the way. Fold over left third of the rectangle toward the center. Sew bottom seam, right sides together (Fig. *j*). Make sure to stitch through only two layers. Add a *kise* fold (Fig. *c*).

8. Open bag and iron seams (Fig. *k*). Take care to keep the *kise* folds intact.

9. Place lining in fabric bag, right sides together. Match seams and pin top edge. Stitch all the way around the top edge (Fig. *m*). Trim seams and clip corners.

10. Turn right-side out through the 3″ opening in the lining. Blindstitch the opening closed. Press.

To use, insert items into the bag and tie a square knot at the top using the long ends. This knot serves as the bag's handle.

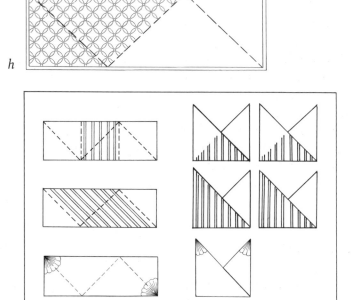

2″ diameter

h

i

j

k   *m*

Alternate pattern arrangements

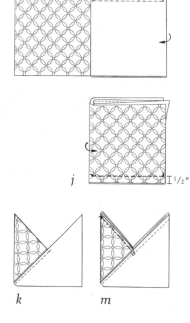

(not drawn to scale)

Floor Cushion (color photo on back cover)

Until recently, very few Japanese households contained furniture that was raised much above floor level. The Japanese sat and slept on the floor, placing nothing but cushions or futon (bedding) between themselves and the floor.

In ancient times, floor cushions were round and made of straw plaited in spiral or concentric-circle patterns. During the Edo period (1600–1868), when cotton and other goods became more readily accessible to the common people, most households began to use 24″-to-36″-square padded cushions covered with cotton, linen, or silk. The square floor cushion (*zabuton*) was probably modeled after cloth-covered straw cushions used by the nobility of long ago; the colors and patterns of the cloth border strips denoted the rank of the user.

Since World War II and the Westernization of Japanese lifestyles, chairs have become popular, but floor cushions still can be found in every home. The cushions are used in Japanese-style rooms in the house when receiving guests, as well as in family rooms for lounging on the floor while watching television. Japanese restaurants also provide floor cushions when guests are seated on the floor and served at low tables.

Since they can be stacked neatly and inconspicuously in a pile in the corner of a room, floor cushions are a convenient way to provide extra seating for large gatherings at home. Sashiko stitching can be used to decorate the cushions and strengthen them as well. While the Japanese tend to change cushion covers to match the season (for example, using linen with water or fan motifs in the summer), you may wish to make one set in colors and patterns that enhance your home interior. A 100% cotton or cotton blend fabric is recommended as it is easy to launder.

MATERIALS (makes one cushion)
fabric: 2⅛ yd* of 15″ width
    OR ⅞ yd* of 45″ or 60″ width
pillow form: 20″ square if purchased, 21″ × 20″ if homemade
thread: red embroidery floss for tassels, white crochet thread for sashiko, and sewing thread to match fabric
*Note: Yardage allows for ⅛ yard shrinkage.

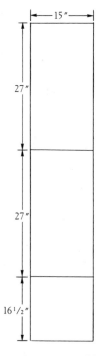

Layout for narrow-width fabric

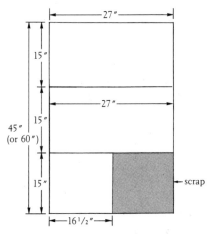

Layout for Western-width fabric

a

1. Cut out two rectangles (each 15″ × 27″) and one "square" (15″ × 16½″). Follow appropriate layout in Figure *a*.

2. Transfer and stitch sashiko design of your choice on 15″ × 16½″ piece, keeping in mind that the finished area that will show is 14″ × 15″ (Fig. *b*). Silk Weave 2 was used here. Or, skip this step and follow step 6 instead.

3. Pin the two rectangular pieces with right sides together and stitch a 1″ seam about 7″ from each end, continuing on toward the top edge at an angle (Fig. *c*). (This angled stitching adds strength when the pillow form is inserted.)

4. Lay the sewn rectangles on a flat surface. Fold down the seam allowance about ⅛″ above the stitching and iron the entire length of the seam (Fig. *d*). (This overlap fold is called a *kise* in Japanese sewing; see also p. 77.)

5. Carefully unfold the fabric. Then, baste through all layers along the opening with large stitches (Fig. *e*). (*Optional:* Sew a zipper or velcro along the opening.)

6. Turn this large square right-side up and stitch sashiko around a 6″ "frame," leaving a ½″ border free of decoration at the edges (Fig. *f*). If center area was decorated with sashiko in step 2, skip this step.

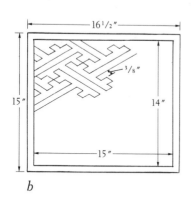

b

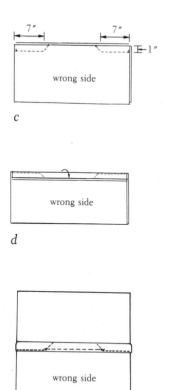

c

d

e

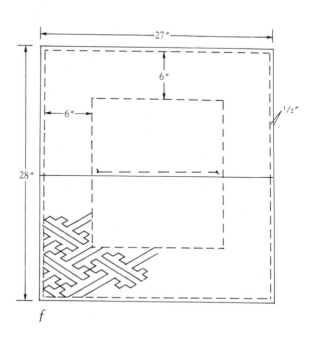

f

7. Fold over each edge of the square 3½" toward the center. Pin fabric on each side of the corners so that this 3½" frame does not move (Fig. g). Do not pin the corners.

8. Working on one corner at a time, fold the excess fabric at the corner to form a triangle and crease the fabric with your fingers (Fig. h: 1). This crease is the seam line. Mark the seam line with tailor's chalk and pin (2). Repeat until all corners are pinned. Sew straight seams from the outer corner stopping about ¾" from the edge of the inner corner (3).

9. Open each corner triangle and press the seam open from the inside (Fig. i: 1). Insert a piece of square cardboard in each corner and press flat (2, 3). Fold back the inner flap of fabric to the outside point of each corner and press (4).

10. Center the 15" × 16½" fabric, wrong-side up, in the middle of the frame by measuring the overlapping sides and adjusting the seam width for evenness. Pin the square piece to the frame, right sides together, on two parallel sides of the frame, making sure all edges are even. Stitch a ½" seam on each side. Repeat for the remaining two sides. See Figure j.

11. Iron seams away from the middle of the cushion cover. Take out the basting from the cover back. Turn right-side out.

12. Insert pillow form, making sure fabric flaps in the corners don't bunch up.

13. Handstitch the opening in back using a tacking stitch (see p. 77). The small stitches will show on the cushion bottom.

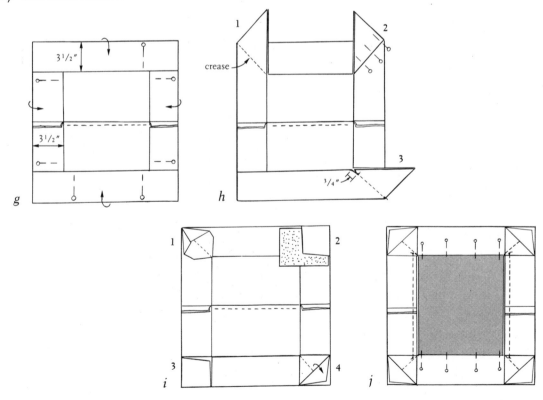

14. Sew a plus-sign shape (+) through the center of the cushion to prevent the cushion from moving within the fabric cover. To do this, first mark the center of the cushion top and bottom with a small plus sign. Measure 1″ from the center of the plus sign and mark the distance with four dots (Fig. *k*).

15. Next thread a needle with a 70″ strand of unknotted red embroidery floss. Align floss ends to make a double strand 35″ long. Following the numbered steps, sew through the cushion using the dots as guides (Fig. *m*).

16. Grasp all threads at cushion top, pull gently, twist the strands together, and then tie the twist into a single knot (like that in Fig. *p*). Cut the tassels 2½″ from the knot and separate the strands of floss.

17. To sew corner tassels, first thread a needle with a 40″ strand of unknotted red embroidery floss doubled over the needle. Insert the needle into the side of the cushion ½″ from the tip of the corner and pull it out the opposite side; then pierce the top of the cushion, ½″ from the tip, and pull the needle out the bottom (Fig. *n*).

18. Twist the strands together and tie the twist into a knot (Fig. *p*). Cut the tassels 2½″ from the knot and separate the strands of floss.

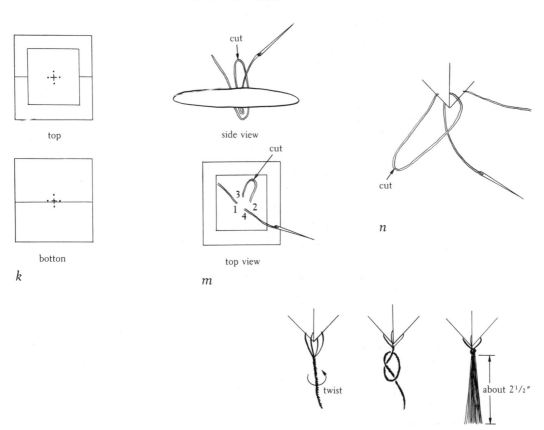

top

botton

k

cut

side view

cut

top view

m

cut

n

twist

about 2¹/₂″

p

Doorway Curtain (color photo on back cover)

Modern Japanese doorway curtains probably originated as one of the many types of partitions used in aristocratic dwellings of the Heian period (794–1185). Interiors of palaces during that time were generally empty except for bare wooden floors and columns. Doorway curtains, screens, and panels of different kinds were arranged to divide the interior into rooms. Some of the curtains were made of raw silk or gauze, depending on the season. Some were padded with cotton for insulation during the winter months.

With the rise of the merchant class around the 1600s, the Japanese curtain became popular as a medium for advertising shops. Storekeepers hung a curtain decorated with pictures of the business's specialty over the entrance to their shops. As society became more literate, the curtain featured the merchant's name and trademark. The shop curtain was hung up in the morning and removed at the end of the business day.

The curtains were made of two or more lengths of narrow-width (14″) cotton or linen cloth, which were sewn together partway down their long sides. The cloth panels parted when people passed through the doorway. These outdoor curtains came in a variety of lengths—from the eaves down to the floor, just down to waist-level, and very short curtains. The curtain provided some protection from the sun, advertised the business name, and more. If the curtain was weathered with age, potential customers could infer that the business was established and reliable, whereas a new curtain advertised inexperience.

Today indoor curtains of various lengths and widths are hung in doorways to bedrooms, living rooms, kitchens, and hallways to separate space, block views, or provide a psychological boundary line. In merchants' homes where the family lives behind the shop, the curtain hangs between the business and private sections of the house. In northeastern Japan, curtains decorated with the hemp leaf or pine bark motif are often included in the bridal trousseau and hung temporarily at the door to the newlyweds' room. In sushi restaurants, very short curtains run between the open kitchen and the dining counter. Short curtains that hang indoors create an illusion of separating space even when there is no real physical barrier present.

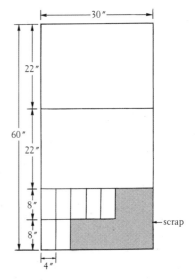

Layout for 60″ fabric

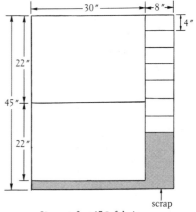

Layout for 45″ fabric.

a

86

In Western homes, Japanese-style curtains can be hung across doorways on spring-action curtain rods or on dowels or lengths of bamboo secured in brackets. Or use double panels bearing related designs as regular window curtains; simply measure to fit the window and don't sew the panels together. Single or multiple panels make attractive decorative wall hangings as well.

To determine the length of a doorway curtain for a particular room, consider the purpose of the curtain. Make the curtain waist-length or longer to block a view (perhaps of a kitchen pantry) or make it short to create a psychological boundary (for instance, between kitchen and dining room). A shorter curtain adds a decorative touch without being a hindrance when, for example, carrying food from room to room. Make the curtain either wide enough to overlap the door frame an inch or two or narrow enough to fit within the door frame.

Finished size: 27″ long × 40″ wide

MATERIALS

fabric: 1¼ yd* of 45″ width
   OR 1 yd* of 60″ width
scrap fabric: 2″ × 5″ piece in contrasting color
thread: pearl cotton #5 thread and embroidery floss for sashiko, and sewing thread to match fabric
*Note: Yardage allows for ⅛ yard shrinkage.

1. Cut out fabric following appropriate layout in Figure *a*.
2. Transfer sashiko design to the two 22″ × 30″ panels. Position design to allow for 1″ side seams, a 2″ hem at the top, and a 1″ hem at the bottom (Fig. *b*).

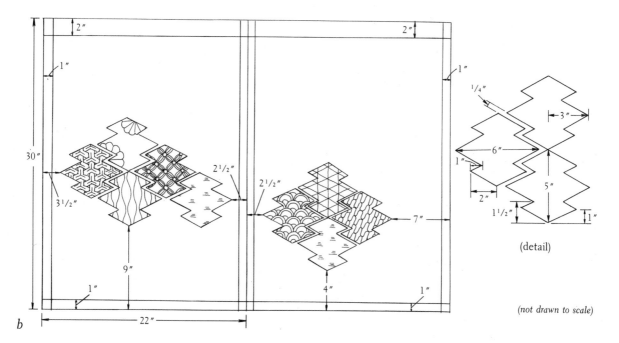

b

(detail)

(not drawn to scale)

3. Stitch sashiko design. Stitch first the Pine Bark outline pattern using pearl cotton, then the other patterns using embroidery floss. Figure *c* shows patterns selected for this example. Since the curtain will be seen from both sides, stitch the patterns neatly. (*Optional*: Cover the knots on the reverse side with fabric cut in the shape of the pine bark lozenges and appliqué it in place.) Press each panel but be careful not to flatten the sashiko stitches.

c

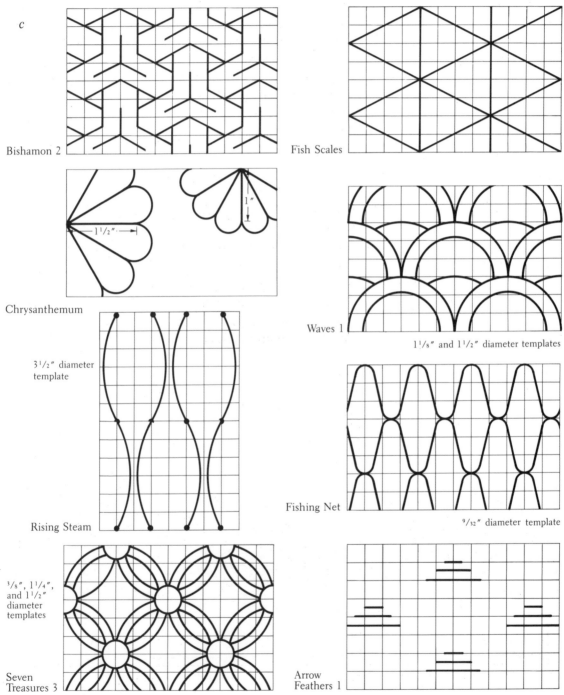

Bishamon 2

Fish Scales

Chrysanthemum

1"

1 1/2"

Waves 1

1 1/8" and 1 1/2" diameter templates

3 1/2" diameter template

Rising Steam

Fishing Net

9/32" diameter template

3/8", 1 1/4", and 1 1/2" diameter templates

Seven Treasures 3

Arrow Feathers 1

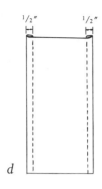

d

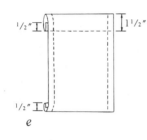

e

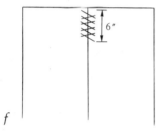

f

4. Triple-fold blindstitch the side seams (see p. 77). Turn each edge under ½″, then under ½″ again (Fig. *d*).

5. Triple-fold blindstitch the hem (turn under ½″ twice) and the top edge (turn under ½″, then 1½″). See Figure *e*.

6. Join panels with 6″ of herringbone stitches (Fig. *f*; see also p. 77).

7. To make loops (Fig. *g*): Fold each 4″ × 8″ rectangle in half lengthwise, right sides together, and sew a ½″ seam down length of strip. Turn right-side out and press, positioning the seam in the center. Press ends ½″ toward center seam.

8. To make bow (Fig. *h*): Cut one 2″ × 5″ rectangle of fabric in a contrasting color. Fold in half lengthwise and sew a ½″ seam at the ends and down the length, right sides together. Leave a 1″ opening in the lengthwise seam. Clip corners, turn right-side out, and handstitch the opening closed. Tie into a simple flat knot.

9. To assemble pieces (Fig. *i*): Fold the loop strips in half widthwise over the top edge of the panels, leaving a 2¼″ loop extending above the panels. Space the strips evenly and pin in place. Stitch the strips to the panels by machine or by hand. Invisibly stitch the bow to the curtain between panels at the end of the herringbone stitches.

10. Add decorative stitching on the strips with thread of a contrasting color (pearl cotton was used here), sewing through all layers of fabric (Fig. *j*). The dotted lines in the illustration indicate the thread positions on the back side of the strips.

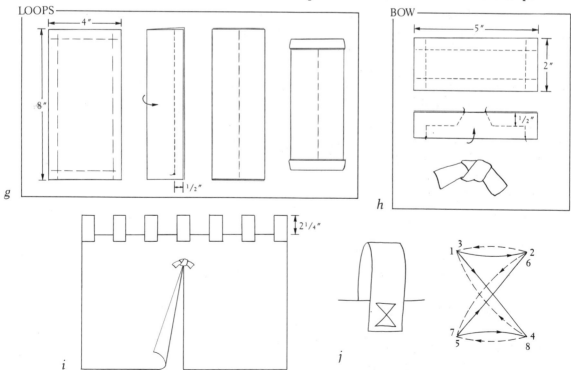

g

h

i

j

Wrapping Cloth (color photo on front cover)

A *furoshiki*, or Japanese wrapping cloth, is simply a square of fabric. Items are placed in the center of the square, opposite corners are folded in, and two or four corners are tied in square knots. The knot(s) formed become a carrying handle. Cloth wrappers range in size from about 12″ to 60″ square, the average size being 27″. Today, countless colors and patterns are used to decorate these cloths.

The use of this handy carryall goes back to sometime between the eighth and twelfth centuries, but the word *furoshiki*, literally "bath spread," comes from a custom that started in the late 1300s. When local feudal lords visited the general's residence, each lord took a square cloth decorated with his family crest to spread on the floor while undressing and to hold his clothes while bathing. Later, commoners began carrying their supplies to the public bathhouses in a square cloth tied at the top.

Nowadays, wrapping cloths are still used to tote things to the bath as well as to store bedding or to carry purchases home from shopping trips. Presents and monetary gifts wrapped in more luxurious squares of silky fabric are ceremoniously unwrapped before being presented to the recipient. The *furoshiki* may double as a shawl, table cloth, or wall hanging. By simply altering its dimensions, the fabric square becomes a handkerchief or coaster, a coverlet or quilt.

Because of the versatility of the wrapping cloth and the unlimited possibilities for sashiko decoration on its flat surface, it is an ideal beginning project.

The *furoshiki* presented here and on the front cover was designed and stitched by Kathleen Sunn.

Finished size: 31½″ × 32½″

MATERIALS

    fabric: 1⅛ yd* of 36″ to 60″ width

    thread: white crochet thread for sashiko and sewing thread to match fabric

    *Note: Yardage allows for ⅛ yard shrinkage.

1. Cut out a piece of fabric 32½″ × 33½″ (Fig. *a*).
2. Make four circle templates with diameters of 7½″, 8″, 19″, and 19¾″. Use these templates to draw (on graph paper) the

Wrapping suggestions

design for the center of the wrapping cloth. Draw four concentric circles radiating from the center (see Fig. *b*). Use the 19″ template to draw the four arcs within the 19″ circle.

3. Draw a "Chinese flower" design (Fig. *c*) inside the 7½″ circle as follows:

—Draw three lines (dotted lines in illustration) that split the large circle into six equal wedges.

—Draw three small semicircles (1, 2, 3), each with a ¾″ diameter.

—Draw two straight lines (each about 2″ long) radiating from the center of each semicircle. These lines should form an 80° angle. Erase the lines that fall within the semicircles.

—Draw large semicircle petals of 1¾″ diameter near the center of the 7½″ circle.

—Draw three smaller petals to complete the sides of each flower. Note that each petal may not be a perfect semicircle; adjust the drawings as you go.

—Finally, draw three ½″ segments that radiate from semicircles 1, 2, and 3.

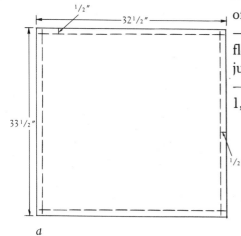

a

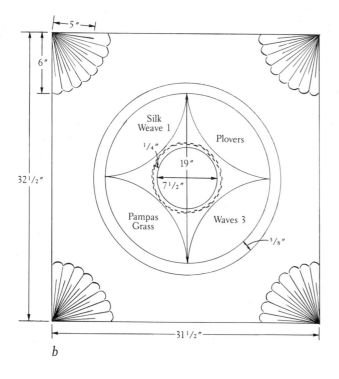

b

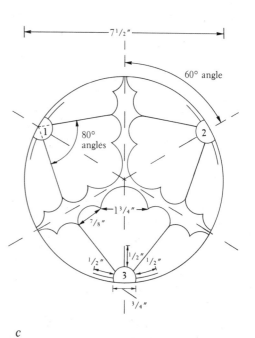

c

4. Draw sashiko patterns in the four scalloped sections around the center circle. Figure *d* shows the patterns used here. Note that a few of the Pampas Grass semicircles are derived from the Bamboo pattern.

5. Draw the corner designs, each consisting of eight chrysanthemum flower petals (Fig. *e*). The measurements are included in the illustration. See the Chrysanthemum pattern (p. 36) for more instructions on drawing and stitching.

6. Transfer all the graph-paper designs to the fabric.

7. Hem the edges of the wrapping cloth with a ½″ hem using a triple-fold blindstitch (see p. 77).

8. Stitch the designs with crochet thread, starting by outlining the circles with a simple running stitch. The 8″ diameter circle is delineated with an outline stitch (see Arrow Feathers 1).

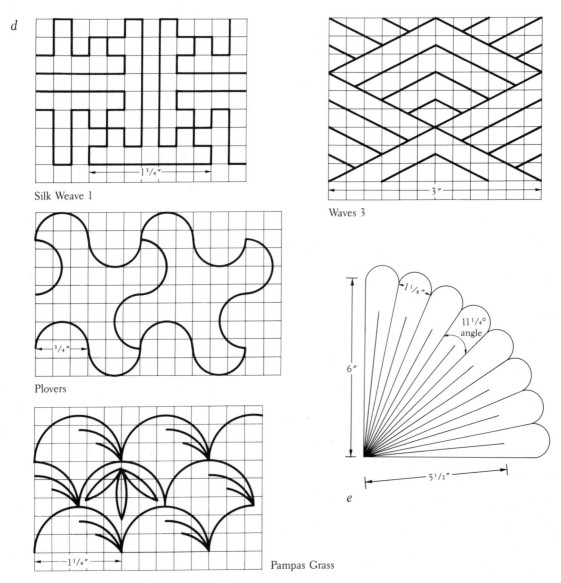

d

Silk Weave 1

Waves 3

Plovers

Pampas Grass

e

APPENDIX 1

Sources of Supplies

AIKO'S ART MATERIALS IMPORT
3347 N. Clark Street
Chicago, IL 60657
(312)404-5600
Hera (scoring tools; called "bone folders" here).

HAKUBUNDO
100 N. Beretania Street
Honolulu, HI 96817
(808)521-3805
Sashiko needles, *hera* (scoring tools), Japanese thimbles.

KASURI DYEWORKS
1959 Shattuck Avenue
Berkeley, CA 94704
(415)841-4509
Narrow-width (14"–16") fabric imported from Japan, sashiko embroidery thread, sashiko pattern stencils (clear plastic), books on Japanese needle arts.

QUILTING BOOKS UNLIMITED
AT THE PRAIRIE SHOP
1158 Prairie Street
Aurora, IL 60506
(312)896-7331
Sashiko pattern stencils (clear plastic with holes), sashiko needles.

TOSHIRO
3309 N. Clark Street
Chicago, IL 60657
(312)248-1487
Ikat and striped indigo-dyed fabric from Japan.

UWAJIMAYA, INC.
P.O. Box 3003
Seattle, WA 98114
(206)624-6248
Sashiko thread, *hera* (scoring tools), Japanese thimbles, wide variety of Japanese craft books.

APPENDIX 2

Bibliography

Adachi, Barbara. *The Living Treasures of Japan*. Tokyo: Kodansha International, 1973.

Brandon, Reiko Mochinaga. *Country Textiles of Japan: The Art of Tsutsugaki*. Tokyo: John Weatherhill, 1986.

Brown, Pauline. *Embroidery*. New York: Villard Books, 1987.

Dunn, C. J. *Everyday Life in Traditional Japan*. New York: G. P. Putnam's Sons, 1969.

Hashimoto, Sumiko. *Japanese Accessories*. Tokyo: Japan Travel Bureau, 1962.

Hauge, Victor and Takako. *Folk Traditions in Japanese Art*. Tokyo: Kodansha International, 1978.

Hayashi, Tadaichi. *Japanese Women's Folk Costumes*. Tokyo: Ie-no-Hikari Association, 1960.

Kaiyama, Kyusaburo. *The Book of Japanese Design*. Translated by Sylvia Price Mueller. New York: Crown Publishers, 1969.

Kawabata, Sanehide. *Nihon Fukushokushi Jiten*. Tokyo: Tokyodo Shuppan, 1969.

Kawashima, Chuji. *Minka: Traditional Houses of Rural Japan*. Translated by Lynne E. Riggs. Tokyo: Kodansha International, 1986.

Koizumi, Kazuko. *Traditional Japanese Furniture*. Translated by Alfred Birmbaum. Tokyo: Kodansha International, 1986.

Lee, Sherman E. *The Genius of Japanese Design*. Tokyo: Kodansha International, 1981.

Lowe, John. *Japanese Crafts*. New York: Van Nostrand Reinhold, 1983.

Marshall, John. *Make Your Own Japanese Clothes: Patterns and Ideas for Creative Wear*. Tokyo: Kodansha International, 1988.

Minnich, Helen Benton. *Japanese Costume and the Makers of Its Elegant Tradition*. Rutland, Vt.: Charles E. Tuttle, 1963.

Mizoguchi, Saburo. *Design Motifs*. Translated and adapted by Louise Allison Cort. Tokyo: John Weatherhill/Shibundo, 1973.

Noma, Seiroku. *Japanese Costume and Textile Arts*. Translated by Armins Nikovskis. New York: John Weatherhill/Heibonsha, 1974.

Rathbun, William Jay. *Yo no Bi: The Beauty of Japanese Folk Art*. Seattle: University of Washington Press, 1983.

Tanahashi, Kazuaki. *Japanese Design Motifs*. Tokyo: Hozansha Publishing, 1968.

Wakamatsu, Masu. *Wafuku Saiho*. Tokyo: Ondorisha, 1966.

Yanagi, Soetsu. *The Unknown Craftsman: A Japanese Insight into Beauty*. Adapted by Bernard Leach. Tokyo: Kodansha International, 1972.

Yoshida, Eiko. *Sashiko Hyakuyo*. Tokyo: Bunka Shuppan Kyoku, 1981.

_____. *Tezukuri no Kurashi: Sashiko*. Tokyo: Bunka Shuppan Kyoku, 1977.

Acknowledgments

I wish to express my heartfelt appreciation to the people who made this book possible: Lisa and Jim Nakata, who showed me the beauty of Japan's traditions and introduced me to sashiko; Ann Asakura, co-founder of Temari (Center for Asian and Pacific Arts), and Jane Neumann, of the Science Museum of Minnesota, for opportunities to teach sashiko; and Gwen Shimono, who gave me a chance to do research on Japanese textiles.

Kathleen Sunn and Pam Jaasko generously shared their ideas and knowledge as expert needle artists. Kathleen, Pam, and Gwen loaned me their stitched creations when I needed inspiration. Kathleen's wrapping cloth graces the cover of this book.

Many thanks go also to Barbara Stephan, who suggested that I write this book and who introduced me to Pamela Pasti. As editor, Pamela orchestrated the elements of the book and guided me from start to finish.

Finally, I wish to express my love and gratitude to my parents, Roger and Edith Watanabe, and to my husband, Owen, whose encouragement, support, and babysitting allowed me to complete this project.